Ray Wharton

Champion In and Out of the Arena

By George Sharman

M. J. Schumacher, Editor

Wild Horse Press

www.WildHorsePress.com

Copyright © 2016
By Frontier Times Museum
Published By Wild Horse Press
An Imprint of Wild Horse Media Group
P.O. Box 331779
Fort Worth, Texas 76163
1-817-344-7036
www.WildHorseMediaGroup.com
ALL RIGHTS RESERVED
1 2 3 4 5 6 7 8 9
ISBN-10: 1-68179-049-1
ISBN-13: 978-1-68179-049-7

Dedication

This book is dedicated to anyone who has had a dream and been told they could not achieve it because they were too poor, too short, not educated enough or lacking in something. Every time Ray Wharton was told he couldn't do something, he worked harder to prove them wrong. He was told he was too short to be much of a roper and he became a World Champion. His own brother told him that poor people like them could never own any land and Ray has owned several ranches and made a fortune buying and selling land. Despite all of the odds against him, Ray never doubted himself. He was always too busy practicing, going to rodeos, training horses, roping and practicing some more to ever question whether his dreams were realistic. He achieved the American dream through sheer determination to succeed coupled with hard work. Just as important to him, he did it while making a lot of friends, helping people in need and having fun along his nine decade ride.

Ray and I had a great life. We were so compatible. We traveled a great amount to rodeos and to see friends. I helped around the ranch as much as a city girl could. Ray always said I was the best fence climber when it came to working cattle. We were so close. I miss Ray dearly.

I'm so glad he decided to share his stories with George and now we can share them with everyone.

Ada Wharton

Contents

Foreword

The definition of the words hustle, try and tenacity are all defined the same way—Ray Wharton from Bandera, Texas. Ray Wharton has two other ingredients as strong or stronger than his hustle—unselfish generosity to help his friends and his genuine, warm and loving personality. Yes, if there was a Hall of Fame for outstanding people in the arena of life, Ray would be a shoo-in.

Randy Moore's Introduction of Ray at his Induction
Ceremony into the National Cowboy Hall of Fame, 1994

Preface

George Sharman was a friend of Ray Wharton's for decades. They visited regularly, especially when Ray's health became problematic. Ray expressed a desire to have a book that chronicled his life. This inspired George to start recording their conversations beginning with Ray's grandparents moving to Texas in a covered wagon and Ray's humble childhood in Kerr County. The makings of the book were finally taking shape after more than two years of taping their weekly conversations, collecting stories and pictures from Ray's friends.

George verified Ray's rodeo statistics at the National Cowboy Hall of Fame and Western Heritage Museum in Oklahoma City, and at the Pro Rodeo Hall of Fame in Colorado Springs.

Dr. Maggie Schumacher, a Bandera resident and writer was brought in at this point to put the material into historical context and book form. Ray and Ada Wharton actively participated in every part of the book. George Sharman and the Whartons agreed that all of the author's proceeds from the book will be donated to the Frontier Times Museum in Bandera, Texas.

Having an oral history that spans nine decades of Texas history and the early decades of rodeo makes this book as remarkable as the subject, Ray Wharton, a true champion in and out of the arena.

Acknowledgments

Many people contributed to this project and we are most appreciative of their efforts. First we are indebted to Ray and Ada who spent an enormous amount of time talking about Ray's life, checking facts, gathering photos and reviewing the manuscript. It is his life story and it is our honor to share it.

We appreciate Holly Boyle who started reviewing the tapes and after seeing the scope of the material encouraged George to turn them into a book. Holly Hasenfratz's support from the Dickinson Research Center at the National Cowboy Hall of Fame and Western Heritage Museum in Oklahoma City was much appreciated. Irene Van Winkle's research on the early Wharton family was invaluable. Thanks also to Rebecca Norton, executive director of the Frontier Times Museum who assisted with the photographs.

To all the people who sent letters about Ray and who encouraged the writing of the book, Thank You! We knew Ray had a lot of friends and your response confirmed this. A special thank you goes to Barbara Sharman for her support of the project and sacrificing her kitchen table for the collection of all of the book's materials. The author's proceeds from the book will be donated to the Frontier Times Museum.

Introduction

The life of Percy Ray Wharton is a story of the American Dream. In 1920 he was born into a family who farmed on the banks of Turtle Creek in Kerr County, Texas. Adversity for Ray began early when his mother died when he was six and a year later when he hurt his right arm, his roping arm. Over the next several years the Wharton family moved from one leased farm to another in the Center Point, Texas, area. Poor is a word they lived every day as they all pitched in to put food on the table.

With a ninth grade education and a deformed right arm, Ray learned to work with his brother Harold. Short, crippled and poor never slowed down Ray. The day Harold told Ray that "poor people like us will never own our own ranch but we'll always work for someone else," was a turning point in Ray's life. That statement lit a fire in Ray as he vowed to prove his brother wrong.

As a young boy the family went to "Uncle" Ed Mansfield's Fourth of July rodeo and barbecue in Bandera, Texas. The stark contrast between farmers and cowboys set in motion Ray's desire to become a roper competing in rodeos.

Even as a young boy, Ray never met a cowboy he didn't like. Ray applied his strong work ethic to his dream of becoming a roper by constantly exercising to strengthen his bad arm and practicing roping anything that moved.

In his late teens he ended up working for Morris Witt who gave him the opportunity to perform in a local rodeo for money. Ray loved everything about the experience. He continued doing ranch work and roping on the side until 1946 when he bought his first horse and then knew he could make a living rodeoing full-time.

Ray always said, "I'm not a cowboy, I'm a gambler. I put up money for the entry fee and try to beat everyone else in the world."

He did just that in 1956 when he won the World Calf Roping Championship. There wasn't a cowboy in the finals who didn't want to see Ray win the championship. Ray's horse Brownie was also part of this endorsement. The little horse was loved by the many cowboys who had ridden him and won money while doing so and they felt Brownie also deserved the Championship title.

In addition to winning the World Championship title in 1956, Ray achieved another one of his goals when he bought his own ranch. Ray always credited his horse, Brownie, for making the ranch a reality.

When Ray was in his fifties, he settled down by raising cows, training horses, participating in jackpot rodeos, and finally marrying Ada Ender, his girlfriend for more than ten years. While Ray and Ada never had any children, Ray raised quite a few young men. Dozens of young men were sent to Ray to help straighten them up or go to jail. Other young men came to the ranch to learn how to rope and train their horses.

Always smiling and ready to have a good time, Ray made friends in all walks of life. The poverty he experienced as a youth made Ray very generous with his knowledge, horses and his own funds. He was always quick to help, often silently, any child he heard of needing medical help. He has also shown exceptional support of his cowboy friends.

Ray freely gave of his time and talents to anyone that wanted lessons about horses, roping and life in general. He was the best friend to have in a fight or a party. George Sharman says, "He wasn't my father, but I sure would have been proud to be his son."

Ray will be remembered for many accomplishments, his sense of humor, and his "try." He is one of the few people who can say, "I've had the best life ever. I've done everything I've ever wanted to do."

Chapter 1

The Wharton Ancestors

Ray Wharton's family tree is as colorful as his own life. After seeing how Ray accomplished so much when starting with nothing, one would naturally question how? How could a man from such poor and harsh beginnings have the wherewithal to say I am going to be somebody despite my size, despite an injured arm, despite members of his own family telling him he would never own his own place because they were so poor. Part of the answer to these questions comes from the courage and "try" of his ancestors.

The Wharton family came to America in the early 1700s while the other side of the family, the Subletts arrived in Virginia in the 1600s. These families survived the battles and poverty in Europe, Scotland and England, the long hazardous voyages across the Atlantic and then more fighting in the young country of America.

The Wharton family story is representative of the families who moved to Texas in the 1800s despite the dangers of Indians and the unknown challenges of the wilderness. The pioneers who made the well documented trips west in covered wagons were hearty self-reliant people. Receiving land grants for service in the army was the way several of Ray's ancestors acquired their properties in North Carolina and Tennessee.

Irene Van Winkle, local Kerr and Bandera County historian, researched the Wharton family for the *West Kerr Current*, as part of a series commemorating the sesquicentennial of Kerr County in 2006.

The William Wharton family came from McNairy County, Tennessee, to Kerr County in 1857 when homesteading was a natural way to acquire land. William and Thankful Wharton settled on 640 acres with their three sons, John Doderidge (1838-1919), William G'laspie (1841-1919) and David Newton

The Wharton Brothers: John Doderidge, left, William G'laspie, right, and David Newton (Ray's grandfather), standing. *Photo courtesy of Susan Sublett Ferguson and Irene Van Winkle.*

(1846-1938), Ray's grandfather.

In an interview from the 1980s one of David's descendants talked about their family's journey west. This interview was reprinted in the *West Kerr Current* (25 Feb 2012) and more recently (12 June 2013) in the Leakey, Texas, newspaper, the *Hill Country Herald*.

David described the trip as taking about fifty days, averaging eighteen miles a day. They had packed two months of food in the wagon which was pulled by three mules and a horse. When they were close to San Antonio, they were warned not to go further west due to the possibility of Indians stealing their mules and horse.

They went back to De-Witt County where they rented land for a year and immediately put in sixty acres of corn. Their efforts produced almost nothing. The discouraged family decided it would be better to move to Kerr County and face the Indians rather than starve. They packed up the covered wagon and journeyed to their original destination.

David, Ray's grandfather reminisced about their first year in Kerr County in a log cabin on Watson Creek. "We spent the first year clearing land and getting a crop started, and then hauled lumber from Kerrville to build a house. We all had the surprise of

Photo of self-portrait painted by Thankful Rankin Wharton, Ray's great grandmother. The miniature was painted in 1826 and remains in the family. *Photo courtesy of Susan Sublett Ferguson and Irene Van Winkle.*

our lives when mother said we could have a dance to celebrate the opening of our new home, mother being an old Presbyterian and very religious."

David would often regale reporters about stories of the camels at Camp Verde just before and during the Civil War. He remembered the names of two of the camel drivers- Mico who is buried on the Herman Lindner farm near Comfort and Hadji Ali, called "Hi Jolly" who eventually moved to Arizona. One humorous story had the camel troop wintering about a mile from the Wharton homestead.

"Horses could smell camels a long distance away and frequently showed signs of alarm at the approach of the tawny, lumbering, humpback animals. When several of the animals came one Sabbath to Camp Ives bringing officers' wives from

Camp Verde, the horses already hitched around the arbor became so frightened and unruly that the minister had to suspend his preaching until the women had dismounted and the horses calmed."

All three brothers worked for Captain Schreiner at the YO Ranch to earn money for the family. Their first jobs were roping and branding cattle. David's brothers, John D. and William G. served in the Civil War in the Confederate forces. David was too young to join the army but he was not too young to work. At the age of fifteen he hauled freight

Photo of Thankful Rankin's gravestone. Born 1803; Died 1887. *Photo courtesy of George Sharman.*

with teams of oxen from the Hill Country to San Antonio, Austin and places as far away as Brownsville in South Texas. These trips lasted a few days to several weeks.

In 1863, David joined Lt T. H. Farr's company of Frontier Rangers and also served in the Texas Calvary. When eighteen, David joined a group of men along the Medina River who were tracking cows that had strayed during the winter. He and the six other men unsuccessfully tried to chase on foot a band of Indians who had stolen their horses. Ray's grandfather, his great uncles and other settlers were more successful chasing off a group of Indians at Bandera Pass while traveling to their homesteads on Turtle Creek.

David Wharton married Susan Melissa Hollimon in 1880. They had eleven children: Alice, Pherby Thankful, Alfred, Oleva, Sidney Lee (Ray's father), Edward Rankin, Mollie Belle, William G'laspie II, Susie Angelina, Gertie, and an unnamed infant.

Dot Young, a granddaughter of David's and a cousin of Ray's, told this story about her uncles. While David never

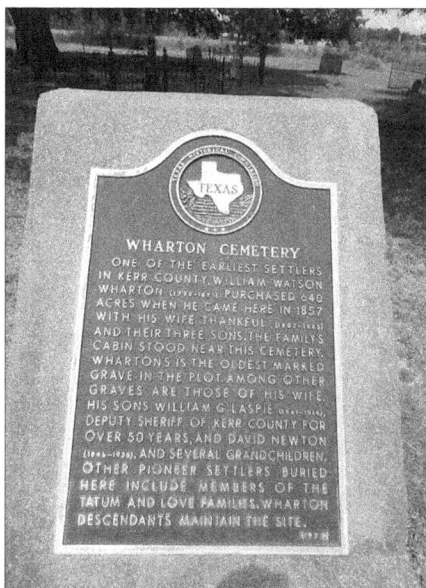

The Wharton Cemetery in Center Point, TX, Historical marker for Wharton Cemetery and grave stones of family members. *Courtesy of George Sharman.*

drank, it is said his brother, William G. or Bill, drank for him.

"Uncle Bill grew up wearing a six-gun. He wore it everywhere and as civilization came to Kerrville, the city council passed an ordinance saying you couldn't wear a six-gun on your hip in town. But Uncle Bill continued to wear one every time he rode in. Now everyone loved him. He was a decent guy until he stopped off at the saloon and got bombed. Finally, the sheriff had no choice but to arrest Uncle Bill for wearing a gun. The problem was eventually solved when the sheriff swore in Uncle Bill as a deputy."

Bill married Lucia Ann Knowlton but the couple had no children. The oldest brother, John, married Rachel McCarty in 1866. They had thirteen children and eventually moved to Oklahoma.

In addition to raising their many children, the Wharton and McDonald families also helped build and establish the Center Point United Methodist Church. The stone structure remains standing today.

Ray's grandparents, David and Susan, lived in their home on Turtle Creek for decades. When David's health began to fail they moved into Kerrville where he passed away in 1938 at the age of ninety-two. He was the last living pioneer in Kerr County on the Confederate Pension Roll.

Chapter 2

The Early Years:
A Rugged Poor Life in the Frontier

Ray's parents were Sydney Lee Wharton and Ruth Margaret McDonald, a descendant of another pioneer family of Kerr County. They had four sons, Harold, Percy Ray, David, and Paul Wayne. They lived on a leased farm next to his grandparents' original homestead on Turtle Creek in Kerr County.

The one room house had a fireplace with a bed placed on each side of it. The kitchen shed and outhouse were behind the home. Water had to be carried uphill from the spring. Sydney Lee or "Pappie" as Ray called him made a yoke that allowed the boys to carry two buckets at a time. The first son, Harold, was born in 1918; Percy Ray was born in 1920 followed by another son, David in 1922. The last son, Paul Wayne, was born in 1926.

The first rodeo Ray remembers going to was when he was four years old. "Uncle Ed" Mansfield held a 4th of July rodeo in Bandera, a well-established tradition that started in the 1920s and lasted more than thirty years. Ray remembers being in awe of the cowboys and studying how they roped. It became the young boy's mission to learn how to rope like them.

Ray often helped his mother with her chores; perhaps because he was her favorite or simply because the oldest brother had to help their father with his outdoor work. Ray's mother went to church every Sunday always taking her sons with her. She taught Sunday school and Ray was in her class. Ray's father knew it was his job to get the horse and wagon ready but he rarely went with them. Their mother made the boys say prayers, kneeling at their beds every evening at bedtime. After listening to Ray's prayers, she made her husband listen to Ray's because instead of saying the traditional prayers, Ray talked to God as he would a person.

"Once I asked for a horse and saddle and I didn't get it. I chewed out the Lord for not getting it. Then Pappie got a little black horse for Harold and me to go to school. I told Harold that was my horse because God gave him to me. I named him Coalie."

After the difficult birth of Paul Wayne in October of 1926, Ray's mother was forced to turn to six-year-old Ray for help. Ruth Margaret was so weak from the loss of blood that as she lay bedridden six days after her baby's birth. She asked Ray to her help relieve the pain in her breasts since she had been too weak to nurse. She asked him to nurse her, spitting out the milk into the parlor pan.

This horrified the young boy and he went running from the house. Margaret Ruth died that night leaving Ray inconsolable. For the longest time, Ray remembered crying every time he heard her name. He blamed himself for not being able to help his mother with her last request of him. Ray carried this guilt with him throughout his entire life, only sharing it with his wife

Early photo of the Wharton boys – back row, left to right, Ray and Harold and two cousins, front row, David. *Courtesy of the Whartons.*

when he knew he did not have much longer to live. When his mother died, Ray stopped praying. In the last week of Ray's life, he cried out to his mother saying he was sorry for not being able to help her.

Typical of the times, neighbors stepped up to help one another. Two neighbor families, Pete Hagin and Buck Nowlan helped Ray's father with farming chores and Mrs. Pervious Jones helped with the newborn, Paul Wayne. Ray thought she was a great cook and one of the nicest women he had ever met.

Buck Nowlan gave Ray his first rope and let him rope his goats that grazed with his Pappie's sheep. Buck had two daughters but always found time for Ray and treated him like he was his own son. Buck became Ray's role model, remembering him fondly saying: "Buck wouldn't do nothin' unless he could do it from a horse."

In the summer of 1927 when Ray was seven, Pappie and his neighbors were harvesting oats. At this time, there were no combines to perform the task. The process involved cutting the stalks and then shocking or putting them in small bundles that would be taken to a thrashing machine, where the grain would be separated from the stalks. The oats would be cut down short enough that rabbits and other small animals could be seen going through the fields looking for food.

Ray was in the newly cut field and looking for their dinner. After chasing and catching two rabbits, he had the two in one hand and was trying for a third when he fell on his right arm. He bruised the bone so severely that it became swollen with infection. After about three days, Dr. Palmer, the local country doctor was sent for and he cut on Ray's arm to relieve the pressure and treat the infection.

This was the first of many attempts over seven years to fix the injury which left his right arm scarred and several inches shorter than his left. Neighbors and family members gave Ray old clothing and sheets that he would tear into bandages. Alcohol and hydrogen peroxide were used to clean the wound and alum powder was sprinkled on it to prevent proud flesh or abnormal growth of flesh around the healing wound. Ray described part of his ordeal.

"Dr. Palmer would probe around to take out pieces of bone that had chipped off. It bled a lot and had proud flesh on it. Doctors said it would never grow again. But I kept using it until it bled, even though it hurt. I did push-ups, and chin-ups and played baseball. I even roped with it. I think that is why it finally healed—because I used it so much."

Ray learned how to clean and bandage his arm, putting three layers on when he played ball so it wouldn't bleed through. When Ray had to do chores that he wasn't fond of, like washing clothes, he made sure blood from the wound could be seen. This got him out of laundry duty until one of his brothers realized they were being duped.

The pain in his arm made Ray return to praying, saying that if his arm could be healed he wouldn't ever ask for anything else for himself.

About two years after hurting his arm, he had another accident. Ray and his brother Harold were racing their horses and Ray knocked his foot on a fence post. Immediately Ray knew that the pain was the same as when he fell on his arm. When he told his father, his father took him to Dr. Secor, a physician in Kerrville.

The doctor operated on his foot right away. This required staying at the hospital overnight which Ray balked at doing. During the night Ray snuck out a window and crawled down a trellis from the second story of the hospital. He intended to walk home to Center Point, a distance of ten miles. His plan was foiled when neighbors saw the young man with one crutch hobbling down the road. Over his protests, they returned Ray to the hospital.

Another experience that left a lasting impression on Ray was when he and a friend were walking to visit a friend. They started to cross the Guadalupe River when the rising water caught the two boys. Ray managed to grab onto a tree limb but his friend was swept away and drowned. This left Ray with a fear of rising water for the rest of his life.

These were the years of the Great Depression in the United States. Families such as the Whartons, who lived out in the country were used to having little, but the harsh economic time provided additional challenges that tested them, but never drained their spirit.

After losing the lease on Turtle Creek, Mr. Wharton and his sons moved to a farm about three miles west of Center Point. When that lease was lost a year later, the family moved back to his grandparents' home. His father took the place of a share cropper.

This move allowed three of the boys, Harold, Ray and David to go to school in Center Point. After the summer of 1930, they moved to Tarpley in Bandera County arriving there after a four day trip across the countryside with their wagon, four milk cows, two horses and 200 sheep.

The land they leased belonged to Elvious Hicks, the sheriff of Bandera County. They built a cedar post barn and Ray built a roping pen. His early start at roping was cut short when attempting to rope a calf; the calf ran off a cliff, broke its neck and died. Ray's father made him tear down the pen and gave him a whipping. In difficult times, losing a calf was a setback; losing an animal to a roping accident was something Ray's father knew could have been avoided.

Being raised around men and with little interaction with women, Ray was left to discover the female world by himself. One day Ray was about ten, he was plowing with four horses near the road when a girl who was about a year and a half older than him stopped and started talking with him. Ray recalls that she wanted to ride the plow with him and he let her.

Later when they were resting under some trees, the girl showed Ray what boys were supposed to do with girls. They met regularly after that, keeping a blanket under the trees for their meetings.

While this story wasn't too much out of the ordinary, what happened twenty-five years later was. Ray was sitting at his table at the Cabaret and this good looking girl walked up to him, sat beside him and started talking.

"You don't know who you're talking to, do you?" laughed

the woman.

Wracking his brain trying to figure out who the attractive girl was and wondering how he could have forgotten such a beauty, Ray answered, "I would like to, but I sure don't."

"Do you remember the girl that used to help you plow at the Wharton Ranch, there on your grandpa's place?" Ray then knew immediately who the woman was. They both had a good laugh about that special time in their younger years.

The boys lived and went to school in Tarpley for four years. Ray worked at the Tarpley ranch herding goats and sheep over the rocky hills and penning them in sheds whenever bad weather came. This work really did not appeal to Ray, but it was their way of life and got Ray to thinking of other ways to earn a living.

During times when corn was ready to be picked, Pappie and the boys would pick corn all morning and afternoon at the Hicks' ranch. Pappie was paid two dollars and the boys were given a dollar each. They were served a full meal at noon with several meats, vegetables and gravy. The meals were almost as important as the wages and were certainly more to their liking than the beans they usually existed on.

During these tough times, going to rodeos or playing ball were the main forms of entertainment. As a young kid he remembers going to rodeos in Center Point, Bandera and other small towns in the area. Ray admits that even as a young boy he just liked being around cowboys.

Ray never had any trouble doing schoolwork until they skipped him from sixth to seventh grade and it was difficult for him to catch up. Blanche Adamietz was his seventh grade Spanish teacher and her brother Buddy was a friend of Ray's. "She made me sweep many a mile for her after school. I broke the broom one time so I wouldn't have to sweep but she made me use the broken broom. I got in trouble a lot, but I wasn't any worse than some of the others."

On one Friday, wanting to get out of school early, Ray was real good all day long. At the end of the day, his teacher asked Ray if he would help sweep the floors. Frustrated Ray blurted out, "Blanche I need to leave early today." She made Ray stay after school that day and every day the next week for calling her by her first name.

For fun Ray played ball with his school friends where his quickness and good eye contributed to his success. Two boys who played with Ray were the sons of Judge Granville Wright, the judge for Bandera County. Judge Wright knew that Ray needed an operation on his arm and knowing that the family could not afford that, he arranged for a grant for the surgery. Ray's father and Judge Wright took him to San Antonio to see a bone specialist at the Santa Rosa Hospital. Ray went on to say:

> They turned me over to the nuns there. They decided to operate on me on my birthday. I was fifteen. I was there ten or twelve days but it felt like a month. I'll never forget the boy that was in the room next to me. He was in a wheelchair and he could drive it better than anyone. I got to riding on the back of it. He could go down the hall faster than anyone, even throwing you off when he turned into a room. He knew all of the nuns, trustees and all of the vacant rooms which made good places to hide from the nuns.

Ray admitted that he turned to prayer again, asking that his arm could be healed. Ray's injury was diagnosed as osteomyelitis, an infection and inflammation of the bone and bone marrow. Trauma to the bone such as taking a hard fall was one of the causes of the disease. While penicillin was discovered in 1928, it was not used in the United States until 1942 thus making treatments for infections like Ray's extremely difficult. Ether was used for anesthesia during Ray's surgery to clean out the infection in his arm but no antibiotics were available.

Despite the fun Ray had cavorting around the hospital with his friend, Ray was eager to leave the hospital. "When they told me to come back in a week or two to take out the stitches," I said, "Doc, I've spent as much time in this hospital as I am going to. I'll take out the stitches myself."

Ray left the hospital in such a hurry that he did not say

goodbye to his friend in the wheelchair who had made his time there bearable. As good as Ray's memory is, he could never remember the fun loving boy's name or where he was from.

Ray was fifteen years-old at the time. If he was giving orders to a doctor at this age, it is no wonder that some of Ray's memories of school include having teachers whom he called cranky, smack the palms of his hands with a ruler. One teacher gave him the assignment to write "I will be good" on the blackboard 100 times. Always thinking and already ingenious, Ray figured out a way to hold two pieces of chalk in his hand at the same time which he figured would reduce his writing time by half. Decades later Ray still remembered Mrs. Bishop as the teacher at Center Point who had regular contact with the palms of his hands.

Ray rode to school on horseback and he used this time to practice roping. One house that he passed had a dog that regularly ran out to bark at Ray. This proved to be too much temptation for Ray so he roped the dog. Witnessing this, the lady of the house, Mrs. Mosty, charged out shouting at Ray. He apologized profusely but then not wanting to get bit, sheepishly asked the woman to take the rope off of her dog. This incident helped

Cedar post barn built by the Whartons in Tarpley. More than eight decades later, it remains standing. *Photo courtesy of George Sharman.*

Ray see the value of charm when dealing with difficult people, especially women.

In addition to the Depression, the 1920s through 1933 were also the era of Prohibition. In many of the small Texas towns, selling whiskey was a common though illegal occurrence during and after rodeos. In 1932, Elvious Hicks, the popular and long serving sheriff of Bandera, was killed by bootleggers at Mansfield Park.

The Whartons leased land from Sheriff Hicks and his death resulted in them eventually losing their lease to Lee Mansfield. They were allowed extra time to stay on the property to allow Ray's arm to heal.

In 1936 the Whartons moved to Red Bluff Creek between Bandera and Boerne. Harold was allowed to go to high school in Bandera. He lived with the Tom Robinson family and worked at their restaurant, Tom's Hamburgers. Harold went to Arizona during the summer and worked for the Civilian Conservation Corps. He earned $21 a month and each month sent $14 home to his father and his brothers. Later Harold worked for Paul Garrison during the summers which would eventually lead to a full-time job.

In 1937 they moved to Utopia and leased a farm that was located near a place ominously named Starvation Canyon. Pappie and his brother-in-law, Addison McDonald, got a loan from the Schreiner Bank on some repossessed sheep. A devastating event happened when the sheep ate a poisonous weed and most of them died.

The boys earned whatever money they could doing odd jobs. Digging post holes for ten cents a hole was one of the jobs Harold and Ray secured. "Someday I'm going to dig holes on my own ranch" Ray told Harold.

His brother, Harold, had a sobering but inspiring response. "You and me will never own any land. People as poor as us will always work for someone else."

This was a turning point in Ray's life. While Ray respected his brother, the thought of him not having his own place lit a fire in him that never went out, often pushing him to work harder and longer than anyone else. Whenever he talked about this, his entire demeanor changed showing his determination to own his own place.

In 1939 the family had to split up after losing the lease in Utopia and going broke. Pappie went to work for Walton Pouge near Rankin, Texas, where they roped with Toots Mansfield. Wayne and David went to Center Point to live with relatives and Harold got a job through Paul Garrison with the new Rural Electric Association. Ray went to work for a short time for a family that lived between Medina and Kerrville.

Ray then went to work for Howard Billings and his son, Felix, helping them build fences and pens. (Felix's son was Clay Billings, who learned to rope on Ray's remarkable horse, Brownie. Years later. Clay went on to become the 1975 Texas State and National High School tie-down roping champion.) This gave Ray his first opportunity to compete in the small rodeos held in the area. Ranchers used the small rodeos to pick out good ropers, knowing this would speed up some of the work with the cattle. Ranchers usually provided the mount and entry fee. When the cowboy won, the rancher received part of his winnings, usually twenty-five percent of the purse for paying the entry fee and twenty-five percent for providing the mount.

Roping was a critical skill for ranchers at this time in Texas as they fought screwworms, larva from blow flies. The flies would land on anything wet, leaving newborn calves particularly vulnerable. Knowing that screwworms could quickly wipe out a herd, ranchers tried to be careful about when their cows were bred so the calves would be born in cooler weather. The calves had to be checked daily for the deadly screwworms. When found, the calves were roped in order to be doctored. After roping a calf, the cowboy tied the calf to a tree allowing them to doctor the calf as often as needed. The mother stayed near her calf so the calf had milk.

Ray often said that he learned half of what he knew by listening. He learned a lot about the economics of rodeoing by observing this method of earning money. He also knew that he had to work harder than others.

"I had this old bad arm so I had to practice a lot. I was pretty stout for a little guy. I used to do push-ups and chin-ups a lot to build up my arm. When I first started I could do three or four but I got to where I could do twenty or so."

Howard Billings always made sure Ray had good horses for him to use at these rodeos. "Old man Billings didn't belong to the Turtles or nothing, but he had a good horse and he roped well, Ray said."

Ray also rode Bush Porter's horse and a horse owned by Bradley Richards that Ray said "fit him real good." At the Utopia rodeo he roped some and even rode bulls. Once he was paid fifty cents to ride a bull and one dollar if he could stay on the bull. In addition to learning more roping skills and gaining a deeper appreciation for good horses, Ray enjoyed the company of cowboys and the rodeo antics.

One time at the Utopia rodeo Ray and a friend were paid to try to ride a bull at the same time. After a coin toss, Ray drew the position of facing forward and the other boy, Lesley Duke, backwards. They didn't last very long but the crowd loved the show and Ray enjoyed the money and the attention from the crowd. Unfortunately for Lesley when he was on the ground, the bull stepped on his leg and broke it.

Ray met Red Hill, foreman of the Woodard Ranch, at the Utopia Rodeo. At the time Mr. Woodard was one of the top ten wealthiest ranchers in the state. Seeing how well Ray roped, Hill offered Ray a job at $30 a month with room and board. Ray worked there for one and a half years.

Mr. Woodard's son, Bob Jr., was going to Texas A&M but when school wasn't in session he worked on the ranch answering to the foreman. Bob Jr. liked Ray and would invite him over for his birthdays, something usually saved for kinfolk. Many years later Ray returned to the Woodard Ranch to help the son, Bob Jr, with their roundups.

One time they had the help of an airplane to find the cattle and even Ray's hat which he kept losing. Ray remembers the pilot being the best he had ever seen, flying the plane so low that it barely missed the top of the trees as he hunted the cattle.

When Ray lost his hat the pilot would find it and holler at him through an old horn and circle the area until Ray found it. One time after roping Woodard's cattle which Ray claimed were the wildest white faced cattle he ever saw, he lost his hat one more time. Bob Jr. was tired of hearing Ray complain about his hat so he took Ray to a store in Utopia owned by J. R. Davenport to buy a new hat. Ray told J. R. to pick out the most expensive hat in the store.

"I thought you said that straw hat wasn't any good," complained Woodard.

"It wasn't but if I'm going to come here and help out at your ranch, I want the most expensive hat this fellow has," Ray replied.

Woodard grimaced at the price though he paid the bill. Woodard never let Ray forget the hat story, kidding him about it and asking him if he still had that expensive hat whenever he could. Their friendship continued for decades.

As the country was going through the Great Depression, the sport of rodeo became a popular source of relatively inexpensive entertainment. It was an exciting time for rodeo as the sport started to be popularly received all over the country. Producers such as Colonel W. T. Johnson, a Texan, promoted rodeos across the country with such flair that it changed the sport of rodeo forever. By 1936, Johnson from San Antonio, Texas, produced the largest rodeos in cities such as Boston, Chicago, New York, Kansas City, Baton Rouge, Houston, and Dallas.

As rodeo became more popular and lucrative, the rodeo cowboys realized they were the ones who needed to speak up for their well-being. The producers were making a great deal of money because of them and they wanted their fair share. Colonel Johnson was taking part of the cowboys' entry fees to use for production costs. A group of cowboys approached Colonel Johnson before the Boston rodeo and asked him to stop this practice. The cowboys wanted all of the entry fees used for the prize money. They knew if Johnson accepted their demands, the other producers would have to follow his lead.

When Johnson refused, the cowboys declined to participate

in the Boston rodeo. Johnson tried to put on the rodeo anyway but it was a disaster. The cowboys were given their demand to double their purses that very night. This "strike" on November 1, 1936 was reported in the Boston newspapers.

RODEO OPENS MINUS STARS

The World Champion Rodeo opened at Boston Garden last night without the world champions—they were all on strike. They had refused to risk their necks in the various events unless Col. W. T. Johnson, producer of the show, would meet their demands of more prize money. Some 65 of the best riders in the country walked out . . . The strikers declared that they had assurances in writing from 130 of the 135 contestants scheduled for the Chicago rodeo that they have no intention of coming here (Boston).

The next day the headlines read: *Cowboys Win Rodeo Strike*. The sixty-one cowboys had watched the rodeo from the stands and heard the crowd booing the poor performances of their replacements. At eleven that night, Col Johnson signed an agreement to pay the men their full purse.

And so the first rodeo cowboy organized group, the United Cowboys Turtle Association, was established in 1936. It was called the Turtles because it took the cowboys so long to form the organization. The cowboys trying to secure fairer purses were led by famed riders such as Rusty McGinty, Eddie Woods, Hugh Bennett, and Everett Bowman. The group would move on to establish written rules governing the events and procedures to get competent judges.

Chapter 3

Working and Rodeos in the 1940s

In 1940 Morris Witt offered Ray a job at his ranch for $25 a month with room and board. He had been getting $30 a month at the Woodard Ranch and was in line to be their foreman, but Morris Witt offered to give Ray a horse on weekends so that he could rope at the local rodeos.

Morris Witt knew Ray from when the family was living at Turtle Creek and Witt sheared their sheep. When Witt took Ray to the Uvalde Rodeo, a sanctioned rodeo, Ray had to join the Cowboy Turtles Association, paying his dues of $5. His number was 1758. This event was significant for Ray though he probably did not realize it at the time.

In an article written by Ray Davis for *Western Horseman* magazine in 1971, he explains how Ray's roping career was different from most ropers of the time.

"Ray was different from most ropers in one way; the majority of rodeo hands or contestants usually compete in several amateur rodeos until they are nearly certain that they can make it at a professional rodeo. Ray has never roped at an amateur rodeo in his life."

Cowboy Turtles Association Pin. *Courtesy of the Whartons.*

With the outbreak of World War II looming and Ray turning twenty-one, he gave his notice to Morris Whit so he could register for military service. Whit gave Ray a bus ticket to Hondo and then Ray hitchhiked to Bandera, the location for registering for the draft. He arrived in

Bandera with a rope bag, two ropes, two pigging strings and one change of clothes. Sitting outside of the OST Restaurant on Main Street, Ray was picked up by Benny Adamietz who took Ray out to his ranch, Bennie's U Bar Guest Ranch.

Ray's arm disqualified him from military service. Through Bennie's help, Ray ended up getting a job at the Mayan Dude Ranch for a dollar a day, board and a cot in the bunkhouse. Bill Morris owned the Mayan at this time. With an arena on the dude ranch, the Bandera Roping Club, a rodeo arena, plenty of horses and calves there were great opportunities to practice roping.

This is how Ray met so many of the local ropers including Toots and Bob Mansfield. Bob Mansfield always made sure Ray had a good horse to ride. Some of the other older ropers tried to discourage Ray about pursuing his roping career because of his size. Telling Ray he could not do something made Ray practice roping even more. In addition to giving Ray a place and time to rope, he entertained the guests when they watched the calves being roped. The job also allowed Ray to go to rodeos on weekends.

On December 6, 1941, Ray went to a rodeo in Waco with Bob Mansfield and the next day, Ray remembers them hearing about Pearl Harbor being bombed by the Japanese. The United States entered into World War II on December 11, 1941.

Still rodeoing only part-time and needing a way to earn some money, in 1942 Ray got a job working with Jim Cravy and Dee Phillips loading trucks with a gravel scoop. The manager told Ray he was too little to shovel gravel all day which of course made Ray shovel faster than anyone else.

Ray then got a job with the Test Fleet Company that had an office in Bandera and Kerrville. He drove the water truck to control the dust in front of the houses on the road between Bandera and Kerrville. They switched to oil because it held down the dust a lot longer. One day he was filling up the truck with oil and it overflowed and oil went all over everything. The truck had a motor on the side of it that was used to pump out the oil. Ray started the pump engine and it backfired and caught the oil on fire. Ray knew the truck had a full load of oil and that he had to do something and quickly. Ray drove the truck into a pond of water to put out the fire. That quick thinking saved the truck, but it also got him fired.

This mishap freed Ray to go to South Texas rodeos with Charlie Montague and Bob Mansfield. One of the events unique to South Texas was steer necking. Steer necking was necessary in South Texas when cowboys on a ranch went after wild yearlings. After roping the outraged animal, they would tie it to a tree and then go fetch a donkey or the lead steer. The animal would be tied to the donkey or lead steer and then dragged back to the corral. In the rodeo version, two men would rope and a third man would tie the rope to a post. Ray typically got the job of tying the steer to the post. Steer necking never caught on in rodeos outside of South Texas.

Charlie Montague's father owned a bank and a lot of land in Bandera. Ray thought Charlie was a great boy and a lot of fun but his father didn't like him running around with Ray and riding Perkins' horses. Ray recalls riding in Charlie's twelve cylinders Buick. "You couldn't drive by a gas station without stopping. It used more gas than you could imagine. It kept me and Charlie broke paying for gas for that thing. Once we went to a rodeo in Robstown. We could see the lights but kept missing the turn. We ended up turning around and went across somebody's yard. "

Jess Perkins, a friend of Ray's, bought good horses from the King Ranch, horses that were fast but not fast enough to run the quarter-mile. Jess always let Ray, Ed and Ralph Arnold ride his horses. At one of the South Texas rodeos Jess introduced Ray to Tom East whose mother was a Kleberg. Tom ran a section of the family's King Ranch. Tom East typically wouldn't talk to anyone unless you could talk "Mexican" but he took a liking to Ray.

Ray recalled:

> Tom asked Jess Perkins about me and he ended up hiring me. We were the only white guys there. Tom was a hell of a nice guy. He had a brother, Robert, who was

just about as far the other way. Tom told me not to tie down any of the calves that Robert brought and to just tie the ones he brought. When I worked there they had about 120 saddle horses. I saw them Mexican cowboys roping their saddle horses from the ground with a low loop and I told Tom, I can't rope those horses like them. I have to swing my loop over my head and I'll run those horses through the fence. Tom called this one little fellow over and told him to rope my horses.

After that he followed me everywhere and we made a pretty good pair. They had this one horse that always tried bucking off his rider. Once Tom caught him but he was hard to get on. Tom warned me the horse would duck one way or another and if he got me off balance, he would buck me off. He did it to me once or twice but I didn't have time to fool with him. Tom told me I didn't have to ride him.

My other two horses had their own problems—one that wouldn't run on flat country where there were gopher holes and the other one would jump at everything when we were in the brush. Those two weren't worth a quarter so I went back to the bucker. I finally got that little horse going and rode him every other day.

We would gather yearlings and young steers that they had missed. Those steers hadn't seen anybody in a year. The first one I roped by the horns. That lil' Mexican cowboy came up and heeled him. I held that steer tight and he got off his horse, held the steer's eyes open and rubbed sand in his eyes. I asked him what he was doing that for and he said when I get through with him, he won't be able to see very good and he'll have to follow the herd. I never saw one you had to do a second time. That Mexican was one of the best cowboys I ever worked with and he sure taught me a lot. We were always working cattle in the pasture. I never saw a pen. We were so damn busy all the time, if you weren't working, by God, you were resting from fighting those wild cattle.

Ray worked there two or three winters catching wild cows and steers, branding and castrating them. Roping in that part of the country had to be done quickly before the steer could escape in the brush. That experience added to Ray's quick and precise roping skills as well as underscoring the importance of having the right horse. Tom East bought a real good blue horse from James Kinney which Ray then took to the Houston rodeo.

In 1945, the Turtles were reorganized and became the Rodeo Cowboys Association (RCA). Their first national headquarters was in Fort Worth. Toots Mansfield, seven-time world champion calf roper, and one of Ray's mentors and fellow ropers from the Bandera area, was the first elected president of the organization. Everyone liked Toots; he had no trouble even in committees. He helped everybody that wanted help. Toots was given card number one in the Rodeo Cowboys Association. He was reelected to the position through 1951 when he resigned. Ray joined the Rodeo Cowboys Association at the Houston Rodeo that year and his number was twenty-six.

After Houston and now a member of the Rodeo Cowboys Association, Ray took to the road to make a name for himself in the roping world. The men whom he rode the rodeo circuit with and the men he competed against would become friends for life. The sharing of rides, trailers and horses, the practical jokes and wild crazy times forged friendships that endured for decades. When a rodeo cowboy married the relationships often "matured" but the camaraderie remained. An example of this is Ray's relationship with Buddy Groff.

Rodeo Cowboys Association Pin.
Courtesy of the Whartons.

Buddy Groff was the first fellow roper to travel with Ray. He knew Buddy from roping at Mansfield Park. One day Ray saw Buddy working in Hondo in a field on a combine and called out to him to go roping with him. Buddy called back and said he would as soon as he got someone to take his place.

Ray came back with his replacement and Buddy jumped into Ray's car. The first rodeo they went to together was in San Saba. Buddy rode Ray's horse Bones and won the roping on him. They traveled together for almost three years.

On their first trip to New York City, their car broke down in New Jersey. Ray opted to stay with the car and horses and sent Buddy on ahead in a bus. The plan was for Buddy to find Toots Mansfield and ask him to borrow his car and trailer. When Buddy got to Madison Square Garden, Toots had already put up his car and trailer. Toots told Buddy to wait and he would find someone to help. Bill Linderman was the next car to come in with his bulldogging horse and a two horse trailer. With Toots asking for help, Bill didn't hesitate, telling Buddy to take his keys and go.

When Ray finally made it to New York, Ray thanked Bill, telling him, "I've got a pretty good roping horse and if you don't have a horse, you can borrow mine and it won't cost you a dime." That was how Bill started riding Ray's horses and it was the beginning of their lifelong friendship.

"One time we were riding together after Buddy started going out with Bonnie and they had gotten cross-ways, Ray said. "I told Buddy to call her up and chew her butt out and tell her to take a swim and to forget about you. We stopped and he called her up. I was standing outside the phone booth. When Buddy came out and saw Ray grinning, Buddy cursed him saying he had done the wrong thing."

Buddy and Bonnie married shortly after that and lived in Bandera where Ray was also living. They stopped traveling together but the jokes continued. One night Ray stopped at the Cabaret, the well-known dance hall on Main Street in Bandera, when Bonnie and Buddy were there.

When Ray left he got in his car that was pulling his horse trailer and headed home. When he got home and was going to put his horse in the barn, Ray discovered there was no horse! Ray called the sheriff, Billy Burns, and told him someone had stolen his horse out of his trailer when it was parked behind the Cabaret. The sheriff said he couldn't do anything until morning which led to a sleepless night for Ray worrying about his horse. The culprit was Buddy who was playing a practical joke on him just to aggravate him and to get back at him for nearly ruining his romance with Bonnie.

Another time Buddy took Ray's horse trailer and parked it on the courthouse lawn. Of course everyone knew it was Ray's trailer and plenty of speculation went on as to how it got there. Ray summed it up by saying "We had some hell of good times."

In 1948 Ray and Buddy went to New York taking Bones as their mount. Bones often jerked down the calves which in New York gave the roper a ten-second penalty. Bones was also a great hazing horse. Ray let other ropers use Bones which eventually took its toll on Bones' speed.

Another horse Ray used was Rusty, Bones' half- brother. Ray often said that Rusty could read a cow's mind. One of Rusty's memorable performances occurred at Cheyenne's rodeo. It had rained so hard that puddles formed in the arena. A calf took off running with Rusty in close pursuit. When the calf approached the puddle of water, he screeched to a stop. Rusty almost ran over the calf. Ray did not place in that round.

Ben Johnson, a fellow roper, reluctantly used Rusty at the St. Paul, Oregon rodeo. Ray gave Ben specific instructions on what to expect Rusty to do. Ray adjusted the stirrups for Ben's height and got them in the roping box. A lot of ropers like to move their horses back and forth in the box but Rusty would not move. At first Ben thought Rusty wasn't ready and he tried to make him move, but Rusty's feet were planted. Ben thought the horse was going to balk.

Ray told Ben to get ready and that as soon as the calf is let go Rusty would know. "He'll straighten out when they open the gate and you hold the rein tight on him. He won't go until you release him, but then he'll take off."

Ben listened to Ray and placed with Rusty. Later Ben went back to Ray and told him he was so sure Rusty was going to balk that Ray could have won every cent he had on him if they had wagered on it.

Ben Johnson was hired by a Hollywood producer to bring horses to California for a movie. Once there Ben was used as an extra which started his acting career. Ray eventually sold Rusty to Jim Bob Altizer, another world champion roper and good friend of Ray's.

In 1949 Ray took a different horse, Cindy, to New York. "Cindy was a good scoring and hazing horse. She worked great on big calves and wouldn't jerk them down. She wouldn't stop or even turn around until you were off and halfway down the rope," Ray said. "Then she would fly back on that rope and hold it steady. She held the rope just tight enough. She was the kind of horse you could win on because you always knew what she was gonna do. Cindy was a small mare so some cowboys didn't give her much respect. Jim Snyder said she was the sorriest horse he had seen in his life, but you're beating up on me."

When Ray told him that he might win something if he rode her, he got madder. Whiz Whisenhunt who had been riding Snyder's horse made things worse by saying he was going to switch to Ray's mare so he could win.

"We did real good in New York on Cindy. T. B. Porter won the average, I won six go-rounds and Leo Brannan won one or two," Ray remembered.

One can imagine the commotion some rodeo cowboys would make in New York City, especially if they were from Texas and named Ray Wharton. One evening Ray, Whiz Whisenhunt, Buddy Groff and Lamar Hinnant took some young ladies including Nancy Bragg and a rodeo queen on a carriage ride through the city. Ray talked the driver into letting him drive the buggy and he proceeded to cut in and out of the New York traffic. One cab driver even yelled at him saying "Cowboy, you're not very long for this town."

When the terrifying ride ended, the real carriage driver shouted, "You're never riding in my carriage again!"

In the late 1940's Ray made a lot of rodeos and ropings with two friends, Buddy Groff and Red Smith. They roped all over Texas, Oklahoma, and made a few shows in New Mexico and Louisiana. As the summer season closed they hauled to St. Louis, Chicago and New York. In 1950 and 1951, Ray won the calf roping at the large San Antonio rodeo. At the close of the season, Ray was in fifth place in the calf roping standings. In 1955, Ray pulled ahead (of Groff) and was in fourth place at the end of the season.

Ray Davis, *Western Horseman*, JAN 1971.

"Pappie" and Ray.
January 1954.
Photo courtesy of the Whartons.

Ray's father, "Pappie" with his Grandmother Wharton. May 1946. *Photo courtesy of the Whartons.*

Ray's grandfather, David Newton Wharton. *Photo courtesy of Susan Sublett Ferguson and Irene Van Winkle.*

Chapter 4
Bandera: Honky Tonks and Rodeos

Bandera: "Cowboy Capital of the World"

"Bandera made guys like me. I never could have become a champion if it hadn't been for Bandera." In turn, World Champions such as Toots Mansfield and Ray Wharton helped to make Bandera the "Cowboy Capital of the World." This mutual legacy was recognized in 1948 by Billie Crowell, editor of the *Dude Wrangler* and owner of the Dixie Dude Ranch. Recognizing the economic benefit of the collaboration of the dude ranches, the rodeos and the cowboys, Bandera was given the title of "Cowboy Capital of the World."

Bandera had so many good ropers, such as seven-time world champion, Toots Mansfield, who were willing to teach younger men. There were many places where they could practice roping such as the Bandera Roping Club and the dude ranch arenas where the local ropers would rope and entertain the visitors. The dude ranches offered employment to cowboys while giving them ample time to practice roping. Bandera was also known as an area with great horses due to its race track. If horses weren't fast enough for the track, they became roping prospects.

It was a way of life that flowed seamlessly for many years. By 1948 there were seventeen dude ranches and nine tourist motel courts in Bandera County. The guests were entertained by watching or participating in ranch activities. Visitors to Bandera loved watching the horse races as much as they loved watching cowboys rope. When dances and music were added, the city and county thrived.

The town appreciated attracting cowboys knowing that their tourist economy was enhanced by their presence. Ray told the story of one of his talks with the local sheriff which demonstrates the laid back atmosphere:

> We practiced roping at Mansfield Park. People let their milk cows roam loose across the highway from the park. I practiced on some of these milk cows and yearlings. Sheriff Billy Burns came up to me and asked me where I'd been practicing roping. He had gotten some complaints about us chasing some milk cows from McGregor's Court across the road to Mansfield Park so we could rope them. We had a lookout, Buck Teich, but he stuttered and especially when he was excited, so he didn't always get the word out in time that someone was coming. I told the sheriff I'd been practicing mostly at the park. The sheriff said 'Well, you better quit at that other place where you've not been practicing.' I knew he knew what we were doing and that was his way of telling us we needed to stop that.

Bandera became the place for rodeo cowboys to live or visit. After the San Antonio rodeos, people flocked to Bandera. It was a great place to train, have your horse trained and a great place to party. This tradition continued for decades. The Gallagher Ranch was one of the popular places that attracted wealthy people from all over the country and the world. Many ropers got their start there roping both cows and ladies. Buddy Groff, Bud Fitzpatrick, and Bill Morris were some of the men who worked there.

Ray regularly practiced roping there, at the Mayan, Lost Valley Ranch and the Flying L. All had arenas where guests visiting the dude ranches would watch the cowboys and where the cowboys could meet young single women guests. Ray was successful in this endeavor too, always getting the names and telephone numbers of women he could visit when he was rodeoing across the country. At the Mayan, Ray always placed his hammock near the main house where the guests checked in thus assuring that he had the first and best pick of the young ladies who stayed there.

One woman who was staying at Bennie's U Bar Ranch caught his attention. Her husband had died during the attack on Pearl

Harbor and she visited Bandera to get a change of scenery. They started seeing one another on a regular basis and created quite a bit of gossip as she left her society life for a rodeo cowboy. The woman was from a prominent Texas family, quite wealthy and visited frequently enough that she had a room held for her at the Lost Valley Ranch and eventually rented her own home in Bandera.

Ray enjoyed many an escapade with this woman but he also cared enough about her to ask her to marry him, even speaking to her family to get their permission. Unable or unwilling to do so because of pressure from her wealthy family, she eventually moved far enough away to not be tempted by Ray's charm.

Ray's rodeo career took a major leap forward when he bought his first horse, Bones. Ray knew early on that "them boys who had good horses won. It makes all the difference between winning and not winning."

Bones was raised by Bob Mansfield and Bob had Ray start him when both were working at the Mayan. "He looked pretty good but he had a bad head on him" Ray recalled. "Bob sold him to Tommy Pyka and Tommy got me to ride him."

When Tommy was drafted into the Army, he left his horse, Bones with Ray. Pyka finished boot camp in 1944 and when he came back to Bandera, Ray bought the horse from him for $500.

Having his own horse that he trained and worked with on a daily basis improved his roping times. Ray taught his horses to drag big cedar logs in preparation for them to drag steers and then stop as soon as you were in place to tie the steer.

Bones was the fastest horse Ray ever rode and with Bones he started winning rodeos which allowed him to rodeo full-time. Ray won the Pecos Rodeo on Bones three times. For years Ray had used other men's horses and now he felt it was only right for him to do the same for others and he always offered his horse to a cowboy in need. Ray also appreciated the economics of sharing the winnings from a cowboy who won using his horse.

"The first summer I hazed on Bones I was asked if Everett Shaw could haze on Bones for them. You had to have a horse that could score any way you wanted him to," Ray explained. "When you were bulldogging you had to have men on each side of the steer to keep him straight. Horses had to score real good coming out like that when you didn't have a barrier. Once when talking about Bones, Everett Shaw told the rodeo boys: 'An old maid could haze on that horse.'"

Bones did have a problem, at times jerking calves down which cost Ray a ten-second penalty in rodeos where this wasn't allowed.

Ray was known for his ability to pick and train horses. Bandera's race track, Lost Valley Downs, brought horse owners and good trainers to the area. Ray made the most of this opportunity by studying the horses and their trainers and always asking questions.

In 1950, Ray was staying in Bandera at McGregor's Court across from Mansfield Park. He built a pen for Cindy, his horse. Ray's father helped take care of the horses but one time he slipped up and Pappie forgot to keep Cindy separated from Buddy's stud horse and she got bred. Cindy was never as fast after that so Ray sold her to Bruce Montague. Despite Cindy's slower performance, Ray came in fifth overall that year.

The next year, Ray bought Brownie from a boy in Quihi, a small Texas town. Ray noticed the horse when he saw a friend of his, "Poochie" Eckhart, riding Brownie at Mansfield Park in Bandera. Ray bought the three-year-old stud for $750 and used him to breed two mares and got two fillies. One of those was bought by Cary Crutcher who made her into a winning show horse. After Ray had Brownie gelded, Brownie slowed down making Ray wonder if he had ruined the horse.

By 1952, Ray was riding Brownie full-time. He was staying at the City Hotel in Bandera between rodeos. At the time Mrs. Alice Faris ran the hotel and owned the OST Café and Soda Fountain, a popular gathering place. Pappie worked at the OST.

There was a group of five girls who ran around with Ray and his rodeo buddies. Ray started traveling to rodeos with Don McLaughlin that year.

With Brownie as a great prospect, Ray decided he could sell one of his other horses. He had bought a "sorry" horse for $100 and spent some time training it. The horse had the aggravating habit of lying down in the arena or in the horse trailer. He had lain down in the trailer twice when Ray was hauling him from Uvalde to Bandera and he stopped twice to get him up. The third time he kept on driving on to the ranch. After fighting with the horse to get him out of the trailer, Ray backed up to a tree, tied the horse's lead rope to the tree and pulled away dragging the horse out of the trailer. "That horse never laid down after that and he ended up making a 'perty' good roping horse," Ray quipped.

He traded that horse to Ralph Mitchell, a good friend, local roper and owner of the Cabaret, one of Bandera's favorite dancehalls, for $1000 and lifetime entry and table at the Cabaret.

At a rodeo in 1954 in Utah, Ray got sick with the flu and was feeling so bad he was put in the hospital. This made the *Hoofs and Horns* magazine which included a reference to Frank Rhoades sending him a bouquet of flowers. Ray insisted that the flowers were really weeds that Frank had picked from the side of the road.

In the same year, *Hoofs and Horns* reported that Ray had donated money for a Bandera boy from the Kalka family to have an operation. Ray also donated fifty-percent of his winnings at a Medina rodeo for football uniforms for the boys at the Medina Children's Home. The next year he dedicated ten-percent of his winnings to help Wally Lawrence get uniforms for the football team of Bandera's Catholic school, St. Joseph's. As Ray rodeoed around the country, he had a lot of young boys keeping track of his winnings.

Roy Rogers was a featured act at many of the larger rodeos. He was able to draw in the crowds especially since he took the time to shake youngsters' hands. Roy would ride Trigger into the center of the arena shooting blanks. One time in Chicago one of Ray's friends was up in the rafters and when Roy shot the blanks, the friend dropped a dead pigeon into the arena. The audience was shocked that their hero, Roy Rogers, would do something like this. Unaware of the practical joke, Roy was mortified. He and Trigger made an early and quick exit from the arena. The humane society did not think much of the joke either.

Ray remembered that Roy Rogers was always real friendly with the rodeo cowboys, even partying with them after the rodeo. Of course when Roy got married, his partying days with the cowboys were less frequent.

The same person who played the pigeon joke on Roy Rogers was also overheard talking with Ray and some Chicago ladies after the rodeo. The giggling girls wanted to know if they were real cowboys. Ray's friend answered, "Yes, ma'am, we're just like our horses; we eat grass and shit while walking."

In 1954 Ray won almost $20,000 with Brownie and almost half of that, including the splits from the wins of the other cowboys riding him, was won in the fall of the year in about sixty to seventy days.

The only thing that Brownie didn't like was Indians. Ray didn't know if it was their drums, their regalia with all the feathers, or what, but it cost him a win at Cheyenne. When Ray's time came up, the Indians who performed at the rodeo were approaching the arena. Dan Taylor was the chute boss and he couldn't understand why Ray was taking so much time to get set. Ray was stalling until the drumming stopped, but just as he went to rope his calf, the drumming started up again, and Brownie spooked. Ray ended up placing third.

Ray and friends partying after a rodeo. Nancy Bragg is in the upper right hand corner, Everett Colburn is the third man on the right, and Tony Salinas is to his right and Ray is on the far right. *Photo courtesy of the Whartons.*

Friends at the Cabaret with Bud Fitzpatrick in the center. *Photo courtesy of the Whartons.*

Ray flipped over his truck and trailer one night near the Hamilton's ranch in Bandera. Photo taken by Mrs. Hamilton the next morning as Ray studies the damage and while her son, George Hamilton, warned her not to lend him their vehicle. *Photo courtesy of George Hamilton.*

An after rodeo gathering- Ray with the white hat. *Photo courtesy of the Whartons.*

Chapter 5
Cowboys, Characters and Champions

Sitting down with Ray and talking rodeo with him is like going through a who's who in the sport. He knew everybody and has a funny story to tell about most. Starting with Toots Mansfield his earliest mentor and his brother Bob Mansfield who taught Ray about horse training, Bill Linderman, Don McLaughlin, Jim Bob Altizer, Lanham Riley, Clark McEntire, Mack Yates—the list goes on and on. Ray made friends with everyone and would help out anyone who needed it. Ray valued these friendships and honored them by making significant contributions in their names to the Justin Cowboy Crisis Fund. *(Appendix 1)*

When asked if Ray realized what a wonderful age of rodeo he starred in, he shrugged it off saying, "We were just busy practicing roping, driving to rodeos, trying to win and then heading off to the next one."

Shoat Webster

Shoat was one of Ray's best friends. Ray met him and Clark McEntire at the Houston rodeo. Shoat roped calves and steers and bulldogged. He was a four-time world champion steer roper winning in 1949, '50, '54 and '55. Similar to Ray, Shoat was known for his exceptional horses especially his beloved, Popcorn.

When necessary the ropers did ride one another's horses. Ray recalls the time when they were in New York and he had put a bunch of boys on Brownie. Shoat was using one of his old steer horses that wouldn't stop so he wasn't winning. At about the next to last go around he drew a good calf. He came over to Ray and said,

"Ray, I'm going to ride that damn brown horse of yours."

No, you're not. You mistreated him the whole time. You're not going to ride him. When they called Shoat's name, he got my horse anyway. When they opened the

Shoat Webster steer roping at Rodeo Finals, 1961.
Photo by Randall Wagner, courtesy of the Dickinson Research Center at the National Cowboy Hall of Fame and Western Heritage Museum, Oklahoma City, OK.

gate and stepped out, he damn near ran over me. He made a hell of a run. I knew he was going to place. I went over to the rodeo secretary and told him that Shoat was going to win some money and he owes me some money so send his check to me. When Shoat talked with the secretary, he said that's right, you send my check to him and his check to me. I had won the average and my check was about three times more than Shoat's. When I called about my check, I learned of Shoat's conversation.

When we saw each other in Del Rio in November at the jackpot roping, Shoat said the only reason he had come was to give me my check. We had quite a deal there trying to switch checks. Everybody got a kick out of us arguing about checks. They knew we ran around together all the time and we were just having some fun.

Shoat was single till he was about thirty-two. We partied a lot up till then. Shoat got crippled at Baton Rouge and he was on crutches. My horse Rusty got sick so I was using Slim Whaley's horse. His little old horse couldn't run like mine so I had to run the calf right to the catch gate before I roped him. I roped him on just his hind leg. I drew up on my rope, flanking him and tied him right by the gate.

Shoat was watching and he said: "You know everybody knows you're a rat, but you're really Mighty Mouse."

Well with all the ropers standing around there, that name stuck for a long time. While we were in Baton Rouge and Shoat was on crutches, he asked me to drive him around to check out some bars and pick up girls. We drove around for a while but didn't see anything interesting. Shoat said that he knew a place that we might try. We pulled up to a pretty big two story house. Since he was on crutches, he had me walk up to the house. A big black woman came to the door and said, "We don't let white boys like you in here.

So I went back and told Shoat that we must be at the wrong house. But Shoat insisted that he was right. So he hobbled up to the house on his crutches and sure enough they ran us off again.

Later on when Shoat got married, he knew sooner or later when I got to know his wife I was going to tell that story. That time came when we were at the Cheyenne rodeo with Tuffy and Jimmy Cooper and their wives who were both named Betty. We were all gathered around and the wives got to asking me questions about Bandera. Shoat's wife, Shirley, was standing there too and she was waiting to tell a story about Baton Rouge. I told her I didn't remember a story about Baton Rouge.

She corrected me saying, "Yes you do. You and Shoat went up to this house and they wouldn't let you in. You went first and then you sent Shoat up on his crutches and they ran him off too."

Oh yes, I remember now. We did that but when Shoat

went up there, they let us in and every one of those girls knew Shoat by his first name. Shirley disagreed saying that's not how Shoat told the story.

Next day when I was watching the rodeo, somebody hit me in the back of the head. I looked around and it was Shoat shouting at me.

"You popping off like that and lying almost cost me a divorce!"

Shirley had been Miss Oklahoma A&M and a Rodeo Sponsor girl so she knew how we kidded around but this joke was a bit much for her.

Ray summed up his feelings about his friend. "Shoat Webster is as good a friend as you could ever hope to have. He was fun to be with and always rode good horses. If you wanted to win any money at a rodeo, you had to figure out how to get around Shoat Webster first."

R. D. Carroll said this of Shoat Webster "No one has ever achieved very much without paying some sort of price. Deserving people are rewarded with a summation of their life and career in books like this."

We believe the same can be said of Ray Wharton. There are many parallels in their lives—how they learned by studying others and then practicing and practicing; their willingness to share their knowledge about roping and horses; both always had young fellows at their ranches who wanted to

Everett Shaw, Cheyenne Frontier Days Rodeo in 1955. *Photo taken by Lucille Stewart, courtesy of the Dickinson Research Center at the National Cowboy Hall of Fame and Western Heritage Museum, Oklahoma City, OK.*

learn how to rope or how to train their horses.

Howard "Shoat" Chouteau Webster passed away in May of 2013 at the age of eighty-eight. He has been inducted into both the ProRodeo Hall of Fame and the National Cowboy Hall of Fame.

Everett Shaw

Shaw was a world Champion steer roper winning in 1945, '46, '48, '51, '59, and '62. He was from Stonewall, Oklahoma. After he quit roping he was flagging in the New York rodeo. He gave me pointers that helped me win a whole lot more. Once after I tied a second calf, he took me down and showed me how I could get my hands up quicker.   I only roped against him one time and he said 'You young guys are putting us old men out of business.' He was a real good fellow. He raised and trained some real good horses. He trained horses for Fred Lowry in Oklahoma. Fred's wife was Aunt Kate, Shoat's aunt.

Shaw hazed on Ray's horse, Bones, and later said "an old maid could haze on this horse."

Royce Sewalt

Royce was another good friend. He won the calf roping championship in 1946 and he was a pretty good bull dogger. He used to come down to Bandera with his wife Maude who kept track of the roping calves. Maude was like a step mother to Ray. One summer they entrusted their son, Ronnye, to Ray

Royce Sewalt at the 1956 Denver Western Finals. *Photo taken by Devere Helfrich, courtesy of the Dickinson Research Center at the National Cowboy Hall of Fame and Western Heritage Museum, Oklahoma City, OK.*

but only after Royce gave him a serious warning saying,—"Ray, he's my only son. Don't kill him."

When driving I didn't stop very much except for gas. One time when I stopped I bought three candy bars. I started eating one and Ronnye didn't say anything. I finally told him he wasn't much company and he wasn't worth a candy bar. I threw the candy bar out the window. That made Ronnye come alive. He was mad but it got him to talking. I did give him the other candy bar. Later when he was grown and in San Antonio with Walt Garrison, he was giving me and Buddy Groff hell. Someone told him that he ought not to aggravate old men like that and he said 'You ought to have traveled with them when you were a kid. They aggravated me to death.' Both Royce and Ronnye were inducted into the Rodeo Hall of Fame. Royce died in 1974 and Ronnye passed away in 1994.

Jim Bob Altizer

Jim Bob Altizer was a real good friend from Del Rio, Texas. Ray asked Jim Bob to ride with him after Jim Bob won numerous junior rodeo titles. They went to rodeos at Vernon, Texas, Cheyenne, Wyoming, Boulder and Colorado Springs, Colorado. He won the national tie-down roping in 1959 and steer roping in 1967. He rode Brownie several times and won money off of him. They continued to have good times at the jack pot ropings in Del Rio, being known as West and Company. Vernon West, Jim Bob Altizer, Mack Yates and Ray were known for walking away with a briefcase filled with their winnings.

Jim Bob Altizer died in December of 1997.

Nancy Bragg

Nancy was a trick rider who began her career on a borrowed horse at the Texas Cowboy Reunion in Stamford, Texas. She was a trained dancer and studied drama at Brenau College. When first starting in the rodeo circuit, the teenager traveled with her mother. Nancy was liked by all of the rodeo people. Ray met her in New York in 1950. He describes her:

Jim Bob Altizer, 1964 at the Pendleton Round-Up, in Pendleton, Oregon.
Photo by Devere Helfrich, courtesy of the Dickinson Research Center at the National Cowboy Hall of Fame and Western Heritage Museum, Oklahoma City, OK.

She was a pretty shiny red headed girl who ran around with all of us. She loved to aggravate me and was always playing pranks. One time she came down to Bandera when they were digging a new water line in town. I had a new car and she got the keys to my new car from either Buddy Groff or Bo Chesson. She drove my car into a ditch right off of Main Street where they had been working on the water line. It was raining like hell and the ditch was about three feet deep. It got bogged down all the way to the axle and a tow truck had to be called to get it out. I was so mad I called the sheriff to report my car stolen. Johnny Faris was sheriff at the time. He told me that the car was stuck in a ditch. I had to get

Nancy Bragg performing one of her amazing acts. *Photo by Stryker Photography, courtesy of the Dickinson Research Center at the National Cowboy Hall of Fame and Western Heritage Museum, Oklahoma City, OK.*

a wrecker to pull it out. They came back the next night and did the same thing. I caught them at Pillows Court. After that I took my keys away from them.

A couple days later Ray was in the Chicken Shack getting something to eat. He overheard two fellows wondering who the fool was who got his car stuck in a ditch two nights in a row. Ray looked up from his table and called over to the men.

"If you want to meet him, it's me."

Nancy would put cigarette butts with lipstick on them in my car to try and make a girl I was seeing mad at me. Her mother didn't like me but that didn't stop Nancy from riding with us. Once in New York she got Bill Hancock and another guy to throw my hat up in the stands. In New York they always made you wear a hat, long sleeved shirts and boots. Nancy knew I would be fit to be tied because I only had one hat.

"You just throwed my hat up there among a bunch of damn Yankees. There's no use trying to get it back." Nancy told me to go up and buy me one of those Gene Autry hats they had for sale. They were small kids' hats.

I went and bought one. When I got to the gate of the arena I told one of the arena police that he had to let me in 'cause I was wearing an authentic Gene Autry hat. Jack Favor was one of the police and he was a big six foot six man. He followed me around until he finally caught me in the clown room.

I got even with Nancy by telling the animal cruelty police that someone was whipping their horse to warm him up downstairs. I told him that she was pretty lively and he would have to be pretty rank with her. Nancy would wave this clapper bat that made a lot of noise around her horse to make him run him up and down the alley to warm up. When the policeman found Nancy, he told her that she would have to pay a fine of $500.He scared the hell out of her and she started to cry. I stepped in and told the policeman that she wasn't hurting her horse with the bat that it just made a lot of noise. Nancy figured out I had set her up so I had hell with her from then on.

Nancy remembers a time in Boston when Ray had booby trapped the box where she put her saddle when traveling. Every time she tried to open it up, she got shocked. After trying this several times, she started looking around and sure enough she found Ray having a good laugh. He had rigged up a line from a hot shot to her saddle box and was turning it on whenever she touched the box.

Nancy Bragg was the featured attraction at rodeos by the time she was seventeen and created the "Falling Tower" act. As an accomplished horsewoman she also won the world champion cutting horse title twice in the Girls Rodeo Association. Nancy Bragg Witmer was inducted into the Cowgirl Hall of Fame in 1997. Even though ill, from her home in Kansas she spoke fondly of Ray and that rodeo era.

"We were more like a family—all of us traveled together or we would all be at the same rodeos. Ray was always happy and full of life. He was fun to be around. He was always polite around women, never cussing in front of us, like some did."

Nancy Bragg Witmer passed away in February of 2014 at the age of eighty-seven.

Casey Tibbs

Casey, a friend of Ray's for decades, was a world all-around champion twice, world saddle bronc champion six times and bareback riding champion once. With their sense of humors and commitment to rodeo they were very much alike.

Ray recalls that Casey would go through town where there was someone he knew and fill up his car with gas and then put it on his friend's bill.

"I told Casey he better not come through Bandera and try to charge anything to me. One day I was driving through town and he was there at Fellows Conoco Station (on Bandera's Main Street) and he had already filled up his car. I came driving by and he hollered at me, 'I'm charging this gas to you.' I didn't stop and sure enough, Charlie Fellows charged the gas to me. Casey had a personality a lot like Whiz. "

When Ray was voted onto the RCA board of directors the

Casey Tibbs on Black Hawk, in the saddle bronc riding at the Red Bluff Round-Up, in Red Bluff, California, 1953. *Photo by Devere Helfrich, courtesy of the Dickinson Research Center at the National Cowboy Hall of Fame and Western Heritage Museum, Oklahoma City, OK.*

year after he won his world championship, they both supported the idea of having a national finals professional rodeo. Ray and Casey were outspoken supporters of this idea. "All the young guys thought we were fixing up a rodeo just for the world champions, because everybody on the board was a world champion. They thought only the older fellows would qualify. But our point system was based on the amount of money you won that year. You could not be excluded if you were eligible. I told them we were doing it for them."

They finally got the support needed and got the National Finals Rodeo approved. Ray spoke of his experience of being on that board: "When I got on the board, I had friends but when I quit after two years, I had a lot of enemies. We were the ones who sanctioned cowboys for hot checks and things like that so you know we weren't popular."

Casey Tibbs died in 1990 in Fort Pierre, South Dakota, at the age of sixty-one. For a man who traveled around the world promoting the sport of rodeo, he ended up being buried very close to his birthplace.

Whiz Whisenhunt

Whiz embodied the carefree rodeo spirit of the early rodeo days. Many of Ray's friends ended up being world champions and have had their lives memorialized through their rodeo accomplishments and families. People often don't remember those who came in third and in the rodeo world that might describe Whiz Whisenhunt if his personality were not so unique. Whiz Whisenhunt was one of Ray's good friends who would merit his own chapter due to his personality alone. Ray often says he was one of a kind and that he was. He also depicts a picture of rodeo life in the 1940s and 50s which shows the good, the bad and the downright crazy.

J. T. Whisenhunt was born in Bonham, Texas, on May 11, 1927. Whiz was a guy that everybody liked. He could get along with the toughest thugs that ever was or the most religious preacher that ever walked. He'd have them all paying attention to him. He played high school

Whiz Whisenhunt steer wrestling at the Sisters, Oregon, rodeo in 1948. *Photo by Devere Helfrich; courtesy of the Dickinson Research Center at the National Cowboy Hall of Fame and Western Heritage Museum, Oklahoma City, OK.*

football and at sixteen also went to rodeoing. He was a bulldogger, calf roper and when he started out he rode bareback and bulls too.

Whiz and another guy came to Bandera one time after being in the San Antonio rodeo and that's when I got to know Whiz real well. There will never be another like him. Boy, he could get you in more storms and get you out of them. He loved to party and could drink with the best and worst of them.

I'll never forget when we finished up a rodeo in Minneapolis and were on the way to New York. We had to drive all night to get there. Dan Taylor, Whiz and me took turns driving Dan's brand new Chrysler and we were hauling a two-horse trailer. Whiz went to sleep and I stayed up and aggravated Dan. We were on the Pennsylvania turnpike just when it was getting daylight and we stopped to eat breakfast. When we finished, it was Dan's turn to sleep and Whiz got behind the wheel and he was laying 'em back. I dozed off to sleep until a siren woke me up. A kinda young highway patrolman pulled us over. Whiz got out of the car knowing he had been going about 100 mph and stormed back to the patrolman.

Whiz asked the cop, 'What in the hell are you stopping me for? Can't you see I'm in a hurry?'

'I can see that pretty plain. You were making ninety miles per hour pulling that trailer you have behind you.'

Whiz told him that we always drove that way in Texas and they never raise hell about it. They were arguing like hell until the patrolman told Whiz to let him see his driver's license.

Whiz said he didn't have no driver's license—'Hell no! I don't got one; I didn't want to drive. Those two fellows back there wanted to sleep and made me drive.'

They kept on arguing and Whiz kept on talking. We just listened wondering how he was going to get out of this. Finally the patrolman gave up and gave him a warning ticket. You can't imagine the things he would think of and say to get him into and out of storms.

Whiz got to be a regular wino; just a damn alcoholic. Every time he got down and real broke, he wanted to stay with me and I'd bring him home. One time I picked him up in San Antonio. He was broke, drunk—been drunk for two months. I told Whiz I had a bar in my old house and I had liquor there. I know how much whiskey I have in the bar and I don't want to see it any lower after I finish drinking. Don't get to drinking and pouring water in it either. Whiz said he wouldn't because he had come out here to get sober. I told him I'd beat him into the ground if he drank my whiskey. He looked at me and said there was no way I could do that. I agreed with him then told him, "I have two big Mexicans out there who will do whatever I tell them. They'll damn sure whip your butt if I tell them to. And don't think they aren't tough enough because they are."   After that talk, Whiz sure sobered up at least for a while.

Once I took him into town to get a haircut. Haircuts were about a dollar back then. Since he was broke, I gave him a dollar.

"I'd like to get it cut all the way around" was his

thank you. He told me to wait for him at the Purple Cow. When I got to the Purple Cow he was visiting with the fellow who owned the Chevrolet dealership. I wanted to get back to the ranch but Whiz told me to go on home. I knew he didn't have any money so he couldn't get drunk so I left him there. It wasn't long before he came driving back to the ranch in a brand new two-door Chevrolet. I asked him how he talked that fellow out of that car. Whiz said he bought it. Bought it, I thought! I knew he had talked that fellow out of that car.

Another time he came down here and after he had sobered up he told me that he needed to use my telephone. I didn't ask why, just told him to keep track of his calls. This was when cattle from Mexico had been turned loose after the quarantine for hoof and mouth disease had been lifted. Whiz knew all the rodeo producers and everybody in the rodeo business. He also knew that they needed cattle. Whiz got in with the Light brothers who had a ranch around Cotulla with a lot of steers. Whiz got on the phone and started calling rodeo producers and ended up shipping steers all over the country. When he returned to the ranch Whiz gave me nineteen one hundred dollar bills. He asked me to keep it for him and if he asked for it to never give it to him. Sure enough there came a day when he called from town and said he wanted some of the money. I told him I lost the key. Then he wanted the banker to open up the safe. That didn't work either. He finally figured out I wasn't going to give him that money until he sobered up. He sobered up and I still didn't let him have any of the money.

One time Whiz had a wreck on the freeway in Houston. It didn't hurt his truck much but he was blocking two lanes. Whiz got out of his truck and went up to the cops and told them he could tell them a lot about the wreck that they didn't know. When the cops asked him who he was, Whiz said that's his pick-up. The police told him to get back in his pick-up and get out of there and stop trying to tell them about the wreck. They ran him off and he was the one that caused the wreck. They got his license number and he had to go to court. When the judge asked him why he left, Whiz, of course, told the truth and said the cops made him leave. The judge told Whiz we need more good citizens like him.

I remember when Whiz borrowed a pick-up that belonged to Cary Crutcher, a friend of mine and Whiz's. Cary was a business man from Houston. Whiz was driving to the liquor store, but he crashed through the front window and drove into the store. The cops called Cary to come get his truck.

"Why didn't you stop?" yelled an angry Cary.

"I didn't know I was there until I passed the cash register!"

Whiz was as popular with the ladies as he was the men. He married three times, once to a wealthy woman rancher from South Texas. He enjoyed living the good life with the rancher woman for a while but when Whiz had a helicopter fly in a pig for her son's 4-H project instead of a calf, their union ended. The pig cost about thirty dollars and the helicopter delivery was about one thousand.

Whiz rode Brownie a lot and placed quite a few times. In 1948 at the Country Onion Fiesta Rodeo in Raymondville he placed in steer bulldogging and roping. He placed in New York a couple of times. None of us drank while we were rodeoing, including Whiz. It was our livelihood and we didn't want to mess up that. Whiz just had a problem when he wasn't on a horse.

A story which shows how endearing the man could be was an incident in Deadwood, South Dakota. Whiz and Vernon Kern were in Deadwood for a rodeo as were some of their friends who participated in the wild west show part of the rodeo. In an effort to promote the event, actors from the wild west show were in town and staged a fight where two fellows were roughing up the woman who played Calamity Jane. Whiz and Vernon were in a bar drinking when they heard the commotion in the street. Seeing their friend Calamity in trouble, they ran over and took on the two fellows and started fighting with them until a laughing Calamity could separate them.

Whiz was good about repaying money he borrowed from Ray. He sent Ray an envelope with ten one hundred dollar bills and this note:

"Sold old Dunny, Ain"t that funny, Look at all the money!"

Ray lent Whiz money in 1954 to buy a horse named Trinket R. Unfortunately, Whiz broke his leg shortly after that and ended up trading the horse for a new station wagon. The mare went on to be an outstanding prospect and Whiz went on to school to learn how to be a radio announcer.

Despite Whiz damaging Cary Crutcher's truck, their friendship stayed intact. When it became obvious that Whiz was losing his battle with alcohol, Cary took Whiz to Houston to help him dry out. While at the alcohol treatment center, Whiz

Bill Linderman, saddle bronc riding. *Photo by the Osborn Photo Studio around 1940, courtesy of the Dickinson Research Center at the National Cowboy Hall of Fame and Western Heritage Museum, Oklahoma City, OK.*

formed a band from men who were there. They often ended up performing for the doctors who were trying to help them with their alcohol problems.

The last time Whiz visited Bandera, he told Ray he was dying. His liver was failing and he didn't have much time left. "But I'll have two of the shiniest angels waiting for you at the Golden Gates" were his parting words to Ray.

Whiz died in Houston on November 29, 1972. He was buried in the New Hope Cemetery in Fannin County where other members of his family are buried. He had packed a lot of living into his forty-five years and has been remembered through various rodeo and ranch associations such as the Stockman's Memorial Foundation and the Justin Cowboy Crisis Foundation. His antics while drinking are legendary but he was also a rodeo cowboy whom everybody liked and he could talk himself into and out of most of the storms he created. Ray often says: "There will never be another like him."

Bill Linderman

Bill Linderman became president of the Rodeo Cowboys Association after Toots Mansfield retired. Toots had introduced Ray to Bill at the New York rodeo when Bill lent Ray and Buddy Groff his car just because Toots had vouched for them. From Montana, he was a large man who rode bulls, bucking horses and bull dogged. He won three world titles in different events in one season. Bill won a total of six world championships in his rodeo career.

Bill roped some too. In New York he borrowed Ray's horse Brownie and placed on his calf winning $204. That same year the RCA board headed up by Bill fined their treasurer, Fred Alley, $500 for rounding up to the dollar the winners' paychecks. All of the cowboys felt bad for Fred and took up a collection to pay his fine. The cowboys drew straws to see who would ask Bill for a donation and Ray drew the short straw.

Ray's request was met with a "Hell No, but here's your check for twenty-five percent of my winnings when I rode your horse. A few years before this when Bill lent his car and trailer to Ray told him he could use his horse and Ray would not charge him. True to his word, Ray never cashed the check for $51.

Years later Bill and Ross Dollarhide were sitting at the Belvedere Hotel in New York and having the young cowboys buy their drinks. Ray saw that Bill was in the bar and before entering he gave all of his money to his date. When Bill saw Ray, he dragged Ray up to the bar and demanded a round of drinks from him. When Ray finished his drink, he said he didn't have any cash, just a check. Bill told the bartender that the check would be okay. When the bartender looked at the check, he told Bill it was a check from his account. Ray had kept the check for seven years. Looking at the check, Bill realized he had closed the account and he was stuck with paying for the drinks.

Despite this Bill and Ray remained good friends. Ray served on the RCA board for two years when Bill was president. Bill died in a plane crash in 1965 doing what he loved—going to a rodeo.

Phil Lyne

Phil Lyne was a great all-around cowboy from Cotulla, Texas where he still lives. Ray, Mack Yates and Vernon West bought a roan horse for Phil in his early rodeo days. Ray said "Phil could beat just about anybody in any event. He could rope them steers and tie em down as good as anybody."

Lyne won the rookie of the year in the PRCA in 1969, winning money in five events. He also won world all-around and calf roping titles in 1971 and '72, as well as a steer roping title in 1990.

In 1972 Lyne won the av-

Phil Lyne
Photo courtesy of Ferrell Butler

erage at the National Finals Rodeo in both the calf roping and the bull riding, an accomplishment no other cowboy has ever achieved in the same year. Lyne has since been inducted into the ProRodeo Hall of Fame and the National Cowboy Hall of Fame.

Scooter Fries

Scooter Fries roped in and around Bandera and had won the Texas High School Championship in 1948 and '51. After that he started riding with Ray on the rodeo circuit.

"Ray was the best teacher and friend a cowboy could ever have. He helped me more than any other cowboy and will always be a friend."

Scooter passed away in 2015.

Lanham Riley

Lanham was a good horse trainer and roper. Ray met Lanham when he got out of the army near San Angelo. Lanham rode Brownie in New York in 1956.

Joe Barnet

He was a big mean looking man who was part Indian. He was a good roper. Joe went with Ray to the Chicago police station when the car

Scooter Fries
Photo courtesy of Sheila Fries

Lanham Riley at the 1958 Denver rodeo. *Photo by Devere Helfrich, courtesy of the Dickinson Research Center at the National Cowboy Hall of Fame and Western Heritage Museum, Oklahoma City, OK.*

Juan Salinas roping at the 1945 Colorado State Fair in Pueblo, Colorado. *Photo by Ralph Russell Doubleday courtesy of the Dickinson Research Center at the National Cowboy Hall of Fame and Western Heritage Museum, Oklahoma City, OK.*

Tom Nesmith (on the right) with Dean Oliver at the 1962 rodeo in Los Angeles, California. *Photo by Devere Helfrich, courtesy of the Dickinson Research Center at the National Cowboy Hall of Fame and Western Heritage Museum, Oklahoma City, OK.*

Ray was using had been stolen. Seeing the officer at the front desk Joe said, "We want to see the son of a bitch who tells you what to do." Ray always appreciated it when Joe had his back.

Juan Salinas

Juan Salinas was an outstanding horseman and owned the great horse Honey Boy. Juan provided Toots Mansfield a horse when Toots first started roping. Through watching Juan train his horses, Ray learned from the best.

Dean Oliver

Dean Oliver was the 1955 champion calf roper from Idaho. Ray and Buddy Groff beat him in 1956. Dean could never understand how that "little son of a bitch" could beat him. Dean went onto win the all-around in 1958, 1960, 1961, 1962, 1963, 1964, and 1969.

Tom Nesmith

Tom was as good of a roper as Ray ever saw. Tom rode Brownie in New York and placed in the average. He stayed

Dean Oliver (on the right) with Benny Reynolds in front of the National Cowboy Hall of Fame at the 1966 National Finals Rodeo. *Photo by Devere Helfrich, courtesy of the Dickinson Research Center at the National Cowboy Hall of Fame and Western Heritage Museum, Oklahoma City, OK.*

with Ray a lot during the San Antonio rodeos.

Gene Rambo

Gene was "one of the best all-around cowboys that walked. He was from California and could beat you at anything. I mean anything. He was one of the toughest rodeo hands I ever saw."

Jimmy and Tuffy Cooper

Jimmy and Tuffy Cooper were from Monument, New Mexico. Both of them had wives named Betty.

"Tuffy rode with me from St. Paul to Oregon. He rode Brownie there and placed on him."

Ray remembers that when Tuffy had to leave his wife and son, Roy, in St Paul, Roy had a fit that he couldn't go with his daddy. Roy's step-daughter married Trevor Brazile, who has twenty-three world championships in rodeo and more than $6 million in career earnings. Roy's three sons have all made names for themselves in rodeo history, with all qualifying for the Wrangler National Finals Rodeo in the tie-down roping. His youngest son, Tuff, has won two world championships.

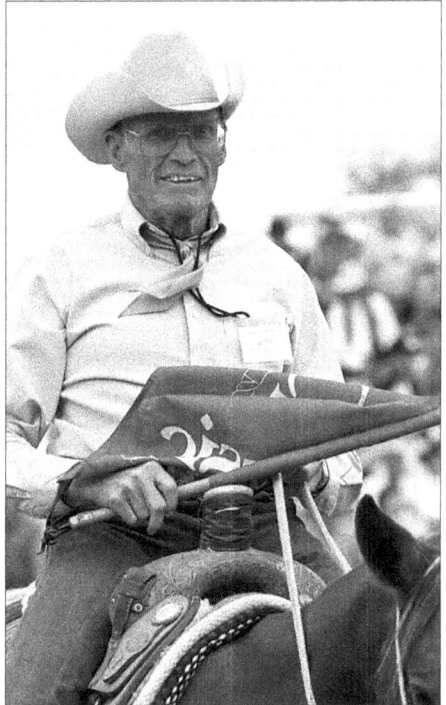

Tuffy Cooper
Photo courtesy of Ferrell Butler

The Coopers were great friends during and after their rodeo careers. For years Ray and Ada met the Coopers at rodeos around the country.

Ray Wharton and Brownie at Billings, Montana, rodeo. *Photos taken by Devere Helfrich, courtesy of the Dickinson Research Center at the National Cowboy Hall of Fame and Western Heritage Museum, Oklahoma City, OK.*

Chapter 6

1956 — Ray and Brownie Earn Their Place in Rodeo History

When 1956 started Ray knew that both he and Buddy Groff had a great chance of winning the world championship. They were both at the top of their game. "I told Buddy, my hauling partner, that if we both get started right and win some good checks this winter, me and you are going to head out and one of us is going to win this roping."

The San Antonio press took note of the promising duo:

Traditionally Texas cowboys would rather rope calves than anything else. And they're better at it, as a rule, than anyone else. Out of the Bandera Roping Club came one of the greatest calf ropers of all time: Toots Mansfield seven times World Champion in 1939, 1940, 1941, 1943, 1945, 1948, and 1950. Two of the younger kids in the club then were Buddy Groff and Ray Wharton who have been roping together "since we been roping" as Wharton puts it. Both big boys now, the two Bandera hands have dominated the national calf roping standings almost since the season began. Groff won the season's first rodeo at Odessa in January; Wharton won the second at Denver two weeks later. And so it went through the year and through the nation. Although it's not uncommon for cowboys to travel together and share expenses, usually the partners hail from different parts of the country. And rarely do they both place among the winners.

San Antonio Express and News, Sunday, Oct 21, 1956.

With Brownie, Ray felt he had the best horse to help him get there. Ray understood that being a great roper was only part of the equation of winning; you needed to have a great horse and you had to work together. Ray rarely had time to think about one rodeo before he went on to the next, sometimes having to leave before he found out the final results. After the rodeo in Denver, Ray was in San Antonio and Red Brown approached him at the Union Stockyard. "Why didn't you tell me you won Denver?"

"I didn't know," Ray said. "I left there right after my last calf."

When at the Lake Charles, Louisiana, rodeo, Lanham Riley told me, "You'll win the championship if Brownie keeps on working and you or your horse don't get crippled."

In September when at the Pendleton Round-Up, Ray got a call to return to Bandera to sign papers to buy his ranch. He flew back to Texas letting Buddy Groff and Marty Woods haul the horses. Another man might have been flustered by this break from routine, but Ray knew buying the ranch meant he needed to win even more. After signing the papers he flew to Missouri to continue his quest.

Truth be told, all the cowboys were rooting for Ray to win. One of his competitors admitted, "There wasn't a man in the finals who didn't want to see Ray win first."

His sense of humor, his generosity toward any roper or rodeo cowboy, his determination to never give up made him a favorite. Brownie was also part of this endorsement. He was loved by most of the cowboys who had ridden him and they thought the little horse deserved the championship too.

After not praying for decades, Ray admits that he did pray for Brownie to not tire out before his run. "Lord, I said I wouldn't ask for anything again, but this is for my horse, not me."

In the 1956 New York rodeo, eleven cowboys rode Brownie during the three weeks of performances. The last performance was the top ten best averages. Six cowboys riding Brownie made the top ten: Lanham Riley, Tom Nesmith, Glen Franklin, Don McLaughlin, Jake Bogard, and Ray.

If Buddy Groff's last calf hadn't gotten loose from the tie down, seven would have ridden Brownie. Others who rode Brownie but did not make the finals were Bill Linderman, Whiz Whisenhunt and Olin Young.

Ray unsuccessfully tried to get the rodeo secretary to let him go first because so many were riding his horse. Ray had the lowest average and had to ride last, but they did let Brownie be ridden on every other calf. Glen Franklin rode Brownie first; Tom Nesmith was second followed by Lanham Riley. Don McLaughlin rode fourth and Jake Bogard was fifth right before Ray. Jake told Ray that he knew he was behind in the average so to give Brownie a rest he would not throw a second loop. All of the cowboys who rode Brownie tried giving him a rest after their roping by slowly walking him back to the roping box. Ray won the average.

Reminiscing about Brownie, Ray said:

Brownie wasn't big and didn't stop hard, but he always held the rope tight when the cowboy went to the calf. Brownie didn't jerk calves so he was perfect for Madison Square Garden where it was against the rules to jerk them down. All the best guys rode him there and in Calgary, another place where you couldn't jerk down calves. You could fly right off of him. If you ever needed to jerk down one of those big calves, you just had to hang in the stirrups and the first thing that hit the ground was the back of the calf's head.

Brownie was sometimes called Scrap Iron because of the nose band Ray had made out of scrap iron. Willard Porter described Brownie in an article for *The Cattleman* in June 1956:

He's so tough and like his rider he's sort of small . . . but also like his rider, he makes up for that with guts, spirit, heart, and the desire to win. He doesn't weigh over 980 pounds, yet he's galloped a lot of ropers to the pay window, including Bill Linderman, Don and Gene McLaughlin, Milton Loper, Shoat Webster, Buddy Groff, Patton and Whisenhunt.

Ray recalled:

I took the lead after New York; only San Francisco was next. Buddy was second. I placed on my first calf and won the championship.

We went to celebrate with Casey Tibbs and Homer Pettigrew. Casey drove us in his Lincoln and took us to the rodeo bar. He left the car blocking the entry. Casey knew everybody and was well liked especially by the photographers. At the gate where you showed your passes to get in, the guards tried to stop us. Casey just ran at them with his big Lincoln and we got through. We all went into the bar, except for Buddy. He waited until we all had a drink and then went and told the cops where we were. Buddy was hoping the cops would give us a hard time, not knowing that Casey was friends with the cops. When one of the policemen came in, Casey threw his keys to the policeman and told him to park the car wherever he wanted it.

After competing in over fifty rodeos in 1956, at age thirty-six, weighing 145 pounds, with one arm two inches shorter than the other, Ray won $21,311 to win the world title. Buddy came in second with $16,551. In those days, that was a lot of money with gas costing about twenty-one cents a gallon and motels running about $5 a night. Entry fees were $25 to $100.

Ray achieved his second goal that year when he was able

to buy his own ranch. Given Ray's humble start, many would have thought both were unreachable dreams.

Ray Wharton and Brownie at Billings, Montana, rodeo. *Photos taken by Devere Helfrich, courtesy of the Dickinson Research Center at the National Cowboy Hall of Fame and Western Heritage Museum, Oklahoma City, OK.*

Ray roping on Bones in New York's Madison Square Garden. *Photo courtesy of the Whartons.*

Ray roping in Houston on a horse belonging to Kenny Call. *Photo courtesy of the Whartons.*

Ray roping a steer at the Cheyenne Frontier Days, July 27, 1956. *Photo by Devere Helfrich, Courtesy of the Dickinson Research Center at the National Cowboy Hall of Fame and Western Heritage Museum, Oklahoma City, OK.*

Ray with his World Champion saddle and belt buckle, November 1956. *Photo by Devere Helfrich courtesy of the Dickinson Research Center at the National Cowboy Hall of Fame and Western Heritage Museum, Oklahoma City, OK.*

Ray after the rodeo in the "Cow Palace" San Francisco, California, November 1956. *Photo by Devere Helfrich, Courtesy of the Dickinson Research Center at the National Cowboy Hall of Fame and Western Heritage Museum, Oklahoma City, OK.*

1956 Champion Cowboys with their trophy saddles in front of the R.C.A. booth at the Denver National Western Rodeo in January, 1957. Left to right: Calf Roping Champion Ray Wharton, Bandera, Texas; Deb Copenhaver, Saddle Bronc Champ from Post Falls, Idaho; Dale Smith, Team Roping title holder, Central Arizona; Jim Shoulders, Henryetta, Oklahoma, with his children Marvin Paul and Jamie, he won All-Around Cowboy, Bull Riding Champion, and Bareback Riding Champion. Harley May, Deming, New Mexico, Steer Wrestling Champion." *Photo by Devere Helfrich, JAN 17, 1957, courtesy of the Dickinson Research Center at the National Cowboy Hall of Fame and Western Heritage Museum, Oklahoma City, OK.*

Ray on the Board of the Rodeo Cowboys Association. After winning the Calf Roping World Championship, Ray became an officer of the Rodeo Cowboys Association. The *Rodeo Sports News*, v.5 no.8 stated that he "has behind him calf roping experience dating back to 1939 and he has been a top hand at it since 1945, and will represent the Calf Ropers well."

1956
Ray Wharton's
World Championship Year Chronology

- **Jan. 3-7- Odessa, TX:** Buddy Groff won the first go-round; Ray placed on one calf.

- **Jan. 13-21- Denver, CO:** Ray placed and won the average. He left for Bandera before knowing results. The San Antonio newspaper announced Ray won and was in first place.

- **Jan. 27- Feb. 5- Fort Worth, TX:** Buddy Groff and Ray placed there. Guy Weeks won the average and went ahead in the standings.

- **Feb. 10-19- San Antonio, TX:** Ray placed first in calf roping and placed 2nd in the average.

- **Feb. 8-12- El Paso, TX:** Cleo Hearn and Ray drove to El Paso. Ray rode Buddy Neal's (1952 PRCA World Champion) horse and won two go-rounds and the average.

- **Feb. 23- 26-Lake Charles, LA:** Lanham Riley and Ray drove to Lake Charles; Ray won two go-rounds. Lanham told Ray: "Keep riding like that and you'll win the championship."

- **Feb. 22-March 4- Houston, TX:** Ray placed on one calf and second in average.

- **March 3-10- Baton Rouge, LA:** Ray placed fourth on one calf.

- **March 8-11-San Angelo, TX:** Ray placed third on one calf.

- **March 30-April 1-Corpus Christi, TX:** Ray won first place.

- **April 14-15- Raymondville, TX:** Ray won one first place and second in the average. Guy Weeks is leading in the standings.

- **May 1-6- Tulsa, OK:** Buddy Groff won first and the average. Ray won second in the average.

- **May 17-20- Shreveport, LA:** Ray won first and fourth and won the average.

- **May 30- June 2- Carlsbad, NM:** Ray won fourth place.

- **June 13- 5- Burkburnett, TX:** Ray won second on one calf and second in the average.

- **June 12-15- Gladewater, TX:** On one calf, Ray won 1st and 1st in the average.

- **June 29-July 1-Elko NV:** Ray won on one calf and placed second in the average.

- **July 1-4- Molalla, OR:** Ray won second on one calf and won the average.

- **July 2-4- Klamath Falls, OR:** Ray tied on one calf.

- **July 9- 14-Calgary, Canada:** Ray won first on one calf and second in the average.

- **July 13-14- Missoula, MT:** Ray placed fourth on two calves and second in the average.

- **July 17-July 21- Nampa, IA:** Ray placed third on one calf. Ray is now in the lead in the standings with Guy Weeks and Buddy Groff placing second and third.

- **July 19- July 24- Salt Lake City, UT:** Ray tied for third on one calf; won the average.

- **Aug. 1-Aug. 4- Spokane, WA:** Ray won second in the average.

- **Aug. 1-Aug. 4 - Idaho Falls, ID:** Ray placed second and third in the rounds and second in the average.

- **Aug. 7-Aug. 11- Great Falls, MT:** Ray won second on one calf; fourth in the average.

- **Aug. 7-Aug. 11-Caldwell, ID:** Ray won second on one calf; second in the average.

- **Aug. 28- Sept. 1-Boise, ID:** Ray won first on one calf.

- **Aug. 31-Sept. 2- Walla Walla, WA:** Ray won third in the average.

- **Sept. 1-Sept. 8- Salem, OR:** Ray placed third on two calves and second in the average.

- **Sept. 7-Sept. 9- Lewiston, ID:** Ray placed second on one calf; second in the average.

- **Sept. 12-Sept. 15- Pendleton, OR:** Ray placed fourth on one calf. Then he flew home to Texas to sign papers for purchase of his ranch in Bandera.

- **Sept. 21-23- St Joseph, MO:** Ray won fourth on one calf and second in the average.

- **Sept. 21-Sept. 30- Omaha, NE:** Ray won third on one calf.

- **Sept. 26- Oct.14- New York, NY:** Riding Brownie, Ray roped six calves winning a third, fourth, fifth, tied for third in the rounds. He won the average.

- **Nov. 2- 4- San Francisco, CA:** Placed on one calf and won the World Calf Roping Championship.

In addition to the prize money, the Pontiac car company gave Ray a new car and he could pay $1,000 every year and trade in his car for a new one. Another one of the side perks for being a world champion was Ray being in a comic strip called *Ride 'Em Cowboy!* printed by Wrangler jeans and placed in the back pocket of their jeans. It was a clever way of advertising their jeans, shirts and jackets. Even his childhood accident with his arm was portrayed with Ray telling the doctor he was worried because it was his roping arm. Another picture shows him practicing roping as a way to get the strength back in his arm.

The comic strip takes him to Madison Square Garden where a boy is asking who's that little cowboy? "Only Ray Wharton, the biggest little rider in the rodeo! The whole rodeo world is rooting for him to do well. He'll make the Biggest Calf Roping Champion Ever!"

Nabisco Shredded Wheat also used this advertising method to encourage eating more cereal so they could get a complete set of the comics. Their last picture had a cowboy with his arm around Ray saying: "There wasn't a man in the finals who didn't want to see Ray win first! That's what we think of him and he deserves it."

Chapter 7

The Ranch

"Poor folks like you and me will never own our own land. We'll always be working for someone else." Harold Wharton told his brother when they were teenagers.

This comment by Ray's brother was a driving force in Ray's life. It had such an impact that during the year of his run for the world championship, he took time out from rodeoing to fly home to Bandera to sign papers buying his ranch.

Ray had been leasing the land since 1952 from Spot Wright. Spot had inherited 776 acres from his father, Judge Granville Wright, the man who helped Ray's father secure funding for Ray's operation on his arm decades earlier. The land had originally been a grant from President Sam Houston to David Harvey for service at the Battle of San Jacinto in 1836.

Ray used the land for a place to put some oversized roping calves and a few cows. He had spent most of those years building fences. When Spot Wright asked Ray to borrow money to pay off gambling debts, Ray agreed using the land as collateral. Logan Adams at the Federal Land Bank gave Ray approval for a loan if Spot's first lien was ever called in. Not being a very good gambler, Spot's troubles worsened and the bank was going to take back the property. Ray got the call about the bank's intentions during the Pendleton Round-Up in Pendleton, Oregon, in September of 1956.

"I told them I had one more calf to rope and then I'd fly home tomorrow. I had the Federal Land Bank loan, all my cash and my car to trade for the ranch," Ray recalled.

Ray arrived in time to show the bank his note for the land and he took over the remaining part of the payments through a Federal Land Bank Loan. At $31 an acre, Ray was able to purchase the 776 acres near Medina Lake that San Antonio and Houston residents found attractive for homes in the Hill Country.

"After taking care of the bank business, I flew to Saint Jo, Missouri, the next day to continue rodeoing," Ray said.

Ray partnered with Fred Morgan a developer who built roads to the lots in exchange for some waterfront property. Ray sold his lots, sometimes loaning the people the money for $10 down and $10 a month for them to purchase the land. He also built Wharton's Dock, helping to pour the concrete himself.

"I made a lot of money that year, especially at New York. I had eleven cowboys riding Brownie at New York and all of them placed and six of them made it to the top six. I made more money getting twenty-five percent of everybody's winnings riding my horse than I did riding on my own, Ray said.

Ray continued roping at big rodeos to earn money to build up his ranch. Riding Brownie, he finished fourth in the standings in 1957. He was also elected to the RCA as the roping director, a position he held for two years.

Never buying anything new, Ray heard that Lackland Air Force base in San Antonio was selling some of their buildings. Ray bought a building and then he, Bill Clendenen, and Jimmy Anderwald moved it in pieces and put it back together on the ranch. He also bought second hand garage doors and built his barn out of them. Jimmy Anderwald made him a horse walker. Ray recalled, "Jimmy could do anything; he was a good hand on horseback and a real good carpenter."

Jeff Moore, a friend of Ray's said, "If there was ever anything I wanted from Ray, it would be in his junk pile. I've gotten some cedar posts that must have been one hundred years old. "

Ray had to keep on rodeoing to make money for the ranch and then he worked on it during the off season. In 1957 Ray met Carl Prelli a young man who had just gotten out of the Army. He wanted a job where he could learn to rope for room and board. Carl stayed quite a while helping Ray build roads, fences and a roping arena. "I'll never forget I had this black horse that was roping pretty good but he would run away with you out in the open," Ray said. "I told Carl it would be best if he led him down to the arena. Carl didn't listen to me and he ended

Pictures of the ranch house and the barn that Ray brought in from Lackland Air Force base. *Photos courtesy of the Whartons.*

up being thrown into prickly pear patch."

Through the years many cowboys and other young fellows lived and worked at the ranch. Some worked for room and board to learn how to rope, some were sent by their parents or sheriff, and some just needed a place to live.

Ray's ranch got to be another popular roping place for Bandera ropers and any other ropers, bulldoggers and horsemen who passed near Bandera.   Bob Woodard, Jim Bob Altizer, Clay and Howard Billings, Bill Murray, Kenny Call, and Logan Adams were just a few of the men who visited with Ray at his ranch.

Carl Prelli, 2014
Photo courtesy of Will Sharman.

When Ray was off rodeoing he had several boys from town live and work at the ranch. Despite his fun loving reputation, he was also known for his serious work ethic and the place was always very busy. Ray never turned down anyone if they were willing to work.

Tom Nesmith came to the ranch to practice roping and he brought Cleo Hearn with him in 1961. Cleo was willing to work for room and board if he could learn how to rope and bulldog. Bill Murray showed up a few weeks later to practice bulldogging and roping.

"We put Cleo in the box on Bill's bull dogging horse and Bill was going to haze for him. I let a steer out and Cleo wouldn't get down on the steer," Ray remembered. "We did it again and still he didn't get down. I told Cleo that if he didn't get down the next time, he would go back to digging post holes. Cleo called us Mr. Bill and Mr. Ray. Cleo said, 'Mr. Ray, that steer will be wearing my black ass this time.' Sure enough, he did."

Cleo Hearn paved the way for many black rodeo cowboys. In 1971, he and three other men formed the Black Texas Cowboys Rodeo. In 1995 the name was changed to Cowboys of Color Rodeo to be more inclusive. In 2009, Cleo was inducted into Bandera's, Frontier Times Museum Texas Heroes Hall of Honor, along with his mentor and friend, Ray Wharton.

Cleo Hearn, 2009
*Photo courtesy of the
Bandera County Courier.*

Tink McCaulley came to learn roping and was having a hard time to get his horse started out of the box. Ray went over to the fence and stood behind Tink and his horse with a doubled up short rope. When the calf broke, Ray whacked Tink across the back with the rope. Tink complained that Ray hit him, not his horse.

Ray answered saying, "But the horse broke out exactly right. Let's try it again."

When Tink and the horse got set in the box, Ray hit him again and again the horse broke perfectly and he made a good rope on the calf. Tink complained again about being hit but he never had another problem starting his horse.

One Saturday morning when they were working horses in the arena, two women drove up to the ranch house. Tink was craning his head around trying to see who they were and what they looked like. Ray told Tink to stay working the horses and he would find out what they wanted. After a few minutes Ray returned and told Tink they were there to see him. Tink went off with a great smile on his face.

The women were from the Jehovah Witness Church and Ray told them Tink would love to meet them. Without learning any religion and without a sense of humor, Tink stormed back to a laughing Ray.

Sonny Greely, Jr. brought a friend named Milford with him to stay at the ranch and practice roping. The three of us would put up a quarter and whoever had the best time on their calf would win the money. Milford was a little lazy but after a day or two, Sonny told Ray that Milford was going to have all of their money if they kept that up.

When his rodeo days were slowing down, Ray stayed involved in the horse business through training horses and the race horse business. Ray typically kept six or seven broodmares. After the time of the San Antonio rodeo he would be visited by some of the rodeo cowboys looking for good horses and he typically sold two or three that way. Other times men would bring their horses to Ray if they were having a problem with them. There were times when Ray would be starting a new prospect and a jockey from the race track would come over and suggest the horse was fast enough to race.

Cabaret was one of these horses. Ray had a couple of mares at his hunting camp where Pappie was living and helped taking care of them. Cabaret had screw worms in his shoulder and they had to ear him down to doctor him. It got to where if you weren't watching, the horse would try to paw at you when you were putting on the bridle.

When he was healed, Ray started working with him at his ranch. At first he thought the horse would be a good roping prospect. A jockey who was learning how to rope saw the horse and told Ray the horse was too fast for a roper and he should try him on the track.

Ray gave Cabaret to Bill Lane, a horse trainer in Bandera. In his first races on July 3, July 17 and August 21, 1966, the horse won. Ray also used Jody Nicodemus and J. W. Speir for trainers. Cabaret continued to win for two years. The only race Cabaret lost was when they had to change jockeys and the new jockey pulled back on Cabaret and he came in third. Ray had a picture of the finish that verifies this story. Ray kept Cabaret for four years and then sold him to a young man in Junction, Texas, who used him as a pickup horse in rodeos.

Ray training a horse at his ranch.
Photo courtesy of the Whartons.

Fencing, pens and chutes constructed by Ray on his ranch.
Photo courtesy of the Whartons.

In 1971, *Western Horseman* magazine did a feature article on Ray's horse training abilities. Ray Davis reported that when Ray agreed to take someone's horse to train, he asked the owner to establish a fixed price on the horse. If Ray decided he wanted to keep the horse after training him, he could buy the horse.

One of Ray's friends said that since Ray had learned everything by studying ropers and horse trainers and then asking questions, he never charged for his training. He did make the cowboys work on his ranch and if they were able to keep up with him, he did his best to help them.

James Kinney, a great horse trainer spoke of Ray, "Everything he knew, he gave away. He never thought of charging to teach someone to rope. He gave pointers to anyone. He would do anything for people who wanted to learn. He loved the sport and was glad someone else liked it. For Ray, you paid for hard work, but knowledge was free."

Ray retired Brownie from rodeoing in the early seventies when his leg started swelling from being hauled around too much. He never limped so Ray used Brownie to help fellows who were learning to rope. Ray lent Brownie to Lanham Riley's son, Kelly, and to Clay Billings for this purpose. Both went on and made names for themselves in roping. He also let Bob Woodard's daughter ride him. Eventually Ray brought Brown-

Cabaret- Start of the race and photo finish, Lost Valley Downs, 1966.
Photo courtesy of Photographic Enterprises.

Photographic Enterprises
Bandera, Texas

LOST VALLEY DOWNS   Bandera, Texas   July 17, 1966   Race 2
Win-Cabaret   330 Yds.   Time-17.72
Owner-Ray Wharton   Trainer-Bill Lane   Jockey-C. Murr
Place-Cariboo Bar   Show-Mr. Sam One

Ray with his race horse Cabaret at Lost Valley Downs, Bandera, Texas, July 17, 1966. *Picture courtesy of Photographic Enterprises.*

ie back to the ranch where he truly retired and spent his days roaming the ranch and eating sweet feed at the Duquettes,' Ray's neighbors.

When Brownie was thirty-one, he went down and could not get up. Ray told his senior ranch worker, Ramon, to put him down. Ramon had been feeding Brownie and thought the world of him. Ramon refused shouting at Ray as he walked away telling Ray to do it himself. Ramon was so mad, Ray thought he might quit. Ray looked at his old friend and knew he couldn't do it either. For all that Brownie gave him and his rodeo friends, Ray knew he had to do right by the old horse. Ray went into the house and called his vet, Steve Sells, and asked him to come out to the ranch and put down Brownie.

There is a stone monument with a bronze plaque at Brownie's grave on the Whartons' ranch. On the plaque twenty-four money winners in RCA and PRCA are listed. It reads as a history of who's who in the roping world of the 1950s, 60s and early 70s. The monument is a fitting tribute to "the horse who bought the ranch."

Jim Bob Altizer tried getting Brownie into the Rodeo Hall of Fame but was told they needed to have his papers to do that. This is the only regret Ray had concerning Brownie and maybe his life.

There are just as many stories about teenagers who were sent to Ray's ranch for some "life lessons." Jesse Evans and Tommy Miller came to work at the ranch while they were in high school. Ray was still on the road a lot but Pappie was living at the house with the boys.

Ray came home one week and the superintendent of the school, Mr. King, called Ray to his office and showed Ray several school absence excuse letters signed by him. Mr. King told Ray that he shouldn't work the boys that hard and he should let them come to school. Ray immediately recognized his father's hand writing and told Mr. King that he would be sure the boys made it to school. Needless to say, Tommy and Jesse talked Pappie into writing the notes for certain trade-offs.

Two Bandera boys, Charley Eckhart who had been expelled

Monument at Brownie's gravesite listing men who won money in the RCA and PRCA while riding him.

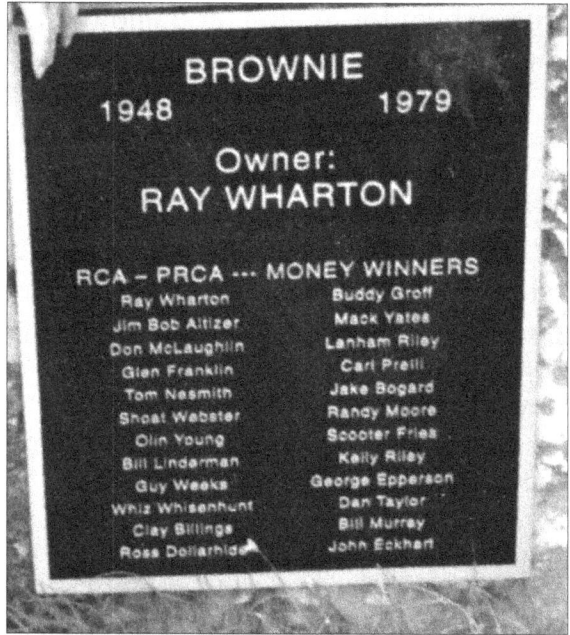

BROWNIE
1948   1979
Owner:
RAY WHARTON

RCA – PRCA --- MONEY WINNERS

Ray Wharton	Buddy Groff
Jim Bob Altizer	Mack Yates
Don McLaughlin	Lanham Riley
Glen Franklin	Carl Preili
Tom Nesmith	Jake Bogard
Shoat Webster	Randy Moore
Olin Young	Scooter Fries
Bill Linderman	Kelly Riley
Guy Weeks	George Epperson
Whiz Whisenhunt	Dan Taylor
Clay Billings	Bill Murrey
Ross Dollarhide	John Eckhart

Portrait of Ray and Brownie at his ranch with his roping pen and Medina Lake in the background, painted by a friend. *Photos courtesy Will Sharman.*

from school for fighting and another boy lived and worked at the ranch. Ray gave them the chore of pulling weeds when he went to town. When Ray returned, Charley explained that after Ray left so did the other boy.

They both got in Ray's truck and found the boy two miles down the road. Ray brought him back to the ranch to finish his job. Ray told Charley, "If he tries to leave again, you whip his butt." That put a grin on Charley's face for a while.

The boy bowed up and told Ray that he would come back some day when he was grown and whip up on Ray. That day never happened.

Years later a young man who had just gotten out of the Navy ran into Ray at Mansfield Park. "Do you remember a boy at your ranch say he was going to come back and whip your butt? " the young man asked.

Ray remembered the incident immediately. "Come on, but remember I don't like coming in second in a fight." Instead of fighting they both ended up laughing as they remembered their short time together.

All of the kids that came to the ranch turned out all right. There was only one I had to send back to Sheriff Billy Burns. The sheriff sent me this kid named Tom. He was difficult and hard to get him to do anything, but I was making progress. Then his mother started visiting him on weekends," Ray recalled. "Every time she came, I had to start over. I sent him back to Billy. One fall I needed help real bad and I hired this boy standing outside the feed store in Comfort. I saw his hands were real white and smooth. When I asked him where he'd been working, he told me he just got out of the penitentiary. I hired him anyway. I had a lot of cattle then that had to be fed every day. He worked all the way up to New Year's and I gave him a few days off. But then he didn't come back. I found him a week later and told him I still owed him some money. He said he wasn't coming back and that 'he'd be better off staying in the penitentiary rather than work for me.'

In the early seventies I rented the ranch house to the two Georges—George Hamilton and George Sharman. They built a barn next to the house from materials I had gotten from Albert Alkek. I had taken down an old aircraft hanger on his ranch for materials. The Georges had been working real hard for a couple of months and I invited them up to the house for dinner. Ada fried up a bunch of oysters and kept the glasses full of whiskey. After a bottle of whiskey, a pack of Camel cigarettes and dozens of oysters, the boys went home around midnight. The next morning I kicked on their door around 6:30 and yelled at them to get to work. I was met with thrown boots and cuss words. That summer they were going to have a barbecue at the house and wanted to borrow my truck to pick up some extra picnic tables. The next day Manuel found some barbed wire wrapped around the drive shaft of my new truck. On the way to town later that day, I saw the fence down on a pasture that John Hamilton had leased. He was out there in the rain fixing the fence and cussing whoever had run over his fence. I told him it was his brother and that other George. The Georges stayed there five or six years.

Just as Ray knew a lot of people from his rodeo career, the same can be said of the people renting his ranch house. The following letters show what an impact Ray had on their lives.

Letter from Ray D'Spain:

I found my way into the Ray Wharton School of Roping, Life's Lessons and Insights into Animals, not having a clue of what lay ahead. I was in college and had made friends with some guys that liked to rodeo. Most of those guys were like me and didn't have money for roping horses or a place to board one. So we rode bulls. I figured out that bull riding was not a healthy sport. I was home for the weekend and telling my parents about my lack of success with the sport. Ray and Ada were over at my parents and Ray told me if I wanted to get involved rodeoing to come down to his arena and he would let me run some calves. I don't think he thought I would take him up on the offer but I couldn't wait to get there. First day I got there, I saw a local roper, Gary Fries, there with a big scab on his forehead. He had been kicked by a gelding that didn't like anyone walking behind him. I just touched the gelding on the rear end and from then on, I stayed clear of his backside. The first time I tried roping, Ray watched me a couple of times and then walked over to give me my first lesson how to tie a calf. He would be calling for time while still pulling the tail of the pigging string through his left hand index finger. Later Ray pulled out a bale of hay and showed me how to hold the rope and how to swing it. Ray had me roping the end of that hay bale and told me if I was throwing my rope correctly the rope would leave a worn spot on the bale. He gave me the hay bale and a good used nylon rope. He had me so hooked on roping, I took that bale of hay with me back to college and stored it in the trunk of my car.

Once he had me work with a 2-year-old filly in a round pen. He put that filly and me in a round pen with a calf and told me to keep the horse's head right on the calf's tail. Then he moved us to a lane and had me roping off of her in a slow lope. Ray walked away when he trusted me not to screw up this part of the training. Things were going pretty well so I figured I would ride that filly into the roping box. Well she balked on me and from there all that progress went the other way. I hoped the horse would get over the experience by the next day, but she wasn't handling right and Ray immediately knew what I had done. I got my first real deal Ray Wharton ass chewing. That filly had a case of box crazy and we had to keep her out of the arena for a long time.

At the end of my junior year in college, I asked Ray if I could live and work at the ranch during the summer. Ray's exact words were: "I'll be glad to have you, but we won't be friends when you leave."

After about a week, we got to the roping pen and I was really liking it. Then I hurt my right knee and I thought Ray was going to shoot me like a crippled dog. But instead he loaned me a knee brace and I kept trying to practice. The knee injury was the end of my calf roping career but I could still ride and Ray had four 2-year-old horses that he wanted to start training. Ray was always more interested in how the horse was working and if he thought you weren't paying enough attention to the horse, you heard about it right then. After about six weeks of riding and tracking calves, the colts were doing pretty well. Ray thought so too because he asked Todd and Ken White-wood, John, Vincent and Mike Teich to come rope off of them. I believe it was Mike Teich who was thrown from his colt as soon as we got in the arena. Not one of those colts even acted like someone had roped on them. Later Ray told me what a sorry ass job I'd done training them. I tried to tell him that they couldn't take that much pressure of being roped off two days in a row, but I was wasting my breath.

Whenever we were traveling Ray had the habit of saying, "We better get a Snickers Bar, we're going to be a while." This meant you should probably get two because we were going to be a long while. It would take me a dozen Snickers bars to tell all that I learned from that man. He is one of a kind."

Due to the length of time Ray spent on each step of training a horse, most of the people who worked for Ray with his horses never saw the complete training program. Just as Ray learned roping by practicing and practicing each step, he did the same when starting a new horse. Perhaps he did this because he knew what had happened to him when he was made to skip a grade in school. He felt he never could catch up and did poorly. He wasn't going to make the same mistake with his horses. Ray was keenly aware of where a horse was in his training and never pushed the horse too far. Ray made sure his roping horses stopped immediately when the rider got off.

And then there was Speedy Hutcheson. Speedy came to work for Ray and became like a son to him. He helped Ray even after he moved to New Mexico by bringing new herd bulls to Ray. Any time Ray called, Speedy was back in Bandera.

Speedy recalled his relationship with Ray in a letter:

I first met Ray when I was about twelve-years-old. My dad and I had gone to Ray's to look at sheep bucks. When we got to Ray's he was working his horse and roping. When we left, Ray invited me to come rope whenever I could.

For the next twelve years, I was at Ray's three to four days out of the week. I guess you could say that was my college education. I didn't actually go to college but I learned from Ray about horses, roping, cattle, ranching, and just life in general. He taught me that if you wanted to be a success in life, you had to make goals, work hard, make commitments and never give up.

I made a fair roper. I won good money in jackpots and in the pro rodeos. I am a Gold Card holding member of the PRCA, all thanks to Ray.

I guess where Ray helped me the most was with my ranching. He sold me my first set of cows on credit. All through the years, if I needed help to buy cattle, he was there. Sixteen years ago my wife and I bought a ranch in New Mexico. It took all we could scrape together, but we needed cattle and once again Ray came to my aid and helped us buy cattle.

For forty-seven years Ray has been there for me. He has been the most positive influence in my life. Ray has a heart as big as Texas, his word is pure gold, and he is a man in every sense of the word. To my friend, Ray Wharton, 1956 World Champion Calf Roper, I appreciate and love you like a dad. I can only hope I have been as true a friend as you have been to me.

Speedy Hutcheson

Ray Davis wrote about Ray's horse training methods for *Western Horseman* in 1971.

Ray has ample pens, chutes and stall in which he can handle young horses. If he feels that a young horse needs some extra handling before he rides him, Ray takes the horse to his large round corral. The round corral makes Ray's job easier, and the horse learns how to move out, stop, and turn in a short time. He does not tie or hobble the horse any more than necessary to handle him. Before the first driving lessons, Ray mouths the horse by letting him carry a snaffle bit for a day or so . . . Ray uses a "turkey track" noseband (a wire noseband that he has made) and a snaffle-gag bit with a chain mouth piece on the horse.

He does not tie the stirrups to prevent them from flopping during the driving lesson; he wants the horse to get used to the motion. He leaves the short, light reins attached to the bit and he ties ropes to the bit and runs them through the stirrups.

Each small step is practiced over and over again. Eventually a calf is added to the corral, then a few steers… If a horse is not working the rope well enough, Ray ropes a few heavier bulls to teach the horse to brace himself in the ground.

As a result of their training, Ray's horses can usually work more than one roping event- and they are thoroughly trained.
Ray Davis, Western Horseman, JAN, 1971.

It was during this time that Ray and Ada finally got married. We felt Ada deserved having a separate chapter, since she had been able to "rope" Ray when so many others had not. But once married they formed such a solid union, it would be difficult to separate her life into a separate chapter. Her background and their courtship are as interesting as the rest of Ray's life is.

Ada's parents were George W. (known as Fred) and Annie Ender from Sinton, Texas, which is north of Corpus Christi. They moved to Bandera in 1951 when Ada was in the seventh grade. After her father's retirement from the post office, Mr. Ender became a justice of the peace. As the justice of the peace and regular church goers, they were respected members of the Bandera community. Ada graduated from high school on a Friday in 1957 and on the following Monday she went to work at the Agriculture and Soil Conservation office where she remained for about fifteen years.

Ray and Ada met in the ASC office. One of their first dates was going water skiing. Ada could water ski quite well though she did not know how to swim. Given Ada's parents conservative background, one can understand that they were skeptical of their youngest daughter dating the older and colorful rodeo roper.

When Ray had a disagreement with the ASC in 1967, Ada

Photos of Ada and Ray.
Courtesy of the Whartons.

quit and went to a position at First State Bank. Similar to high school, she left the position on a Friday and was working at her new job on the next Monday.

Their mutual friend, Beatrice Poe, who worked at the bank with Ada, told Ray that he needed an accountant to track all of his real estate deals. But then she suggested that he should marry Ada since she was a great bookkeeper.

Ray responded with one of his classic statements: "I've been married three or four times. We drive down to Mexico, get the license and then when we are returning, I throw away the license before we cross into Texas."

Ada overheard Ray bantering with Beatrice and believing him, she filed away that information. The couple saw one another for about ten years and then decided to live together. Knowing that the ranch house wouldn't suit a couple, Ray decided to move Ada into a house on Lake Medina that he had bought from Colonel Jones.

Ray packed Ada's possessions in a pick-up and was going to "slip" over to the house but had a barking dog as their escort. Ada did not realize her possessions were being moved until she looked out the bank's window and saw Ray, a pick-up with her belongings and her dog all going down the street.

Living together just outside of a small town was the exception for the times. Ray said that he wanted to be sure he was making the right decision when he got married.

In 1970 they finally made the decision to get married by going to Mexico. They went alone but ran into two Bandera couples, Dr. Meador and his wife and the Montagues. When the newlyweds were returning to Texas, Ada remembered Ray saying what he had done with other marriage certificates so she held onto the paper. At home she put it away in a safe. More than forty years later, the marriage certificate remains in Ada's safe.

On their first anniversary, Ada bought Ray a small present and set it on the coffee table. Being a child of the Depression, Ray was never big on gifts and he told her that he wasn't going to open it. One Christmas, Ray did get Ada a present but he signed it from Manuel, their ranch manager and his family. Seeing that the family had gotten her a gift, Ada went out and bought all of them Christmas presents. On Christmas day when she opened the present and saw a fancy watch, she realized it was from Ray. She thought it was too pretty to wear so kept it in its box.

Ada's mother passed away in 1977 and Pappie died in 1979. He was buried in Center Point next to his wife who had died more than fifty years earlier.

Ada continued to work at the bank until 1981. When she retired they were able to travel more visiting friends, going to rodeos and reunions. Friends have said that she was the only woman in the world who could have put up with Ray over the long haul. She probably was the only man or woman to be able to make Ray stop complaining.

Once he started fussing about her bookkeeping and she quickly cut him off saying his bank account had not seen any red ink since she started managing the books. For more than forty years they took care of one another and Ada deserves a championship buckle for that accomplishment.

Shirley Almond, a woman originally from England who lived at the ranch for a few years offered her comments in a letter about the time she lived at the ranch.

> *I always said I watched too many westerns thirty years ago which made me want to come to Texas. I had brought horses to Bandera to work them and always said I wanted to live there. I had heard about Ray Wharton and he made me an offer to rent a place where I could have my horses and dogs where I could work off my rent. I also found a full time job working for a vet. It was a lot of long hard days. Once I needed to sell a horse and Ray and I wheeled and dealed back and forth on the price. Well, you can guess who won that one. Ray had race horses and I was supposed to halter break them. We tied them to the truck and off we went, dust flying. It sure was different from how we halter broke horses in the UK, but after one ride with Ray's truck, the horses never pulled back.*
>
> *His round pen was held together with baling wire and he*

made me a whip out of baling wire. I should have kept that for a souvenir. When we messed up Ray's favorite word was "god dammit." A lot of people came there to better themselves in calf roping. Ray always told the fellows how they were doing, even if they didn't want to hear it. I always wished I could have learned to rope from Ray. I would have had the best teacher. We never had a dull moment. It was a lot of adventures and good times.

Shirley Almond

After Shirley left the ranch, another person from England, Gordon Prest, moved in with his family. Gordon had never ridden a horse. He was a good mechanic and learned to drive a bulldozer and was able to move a lot of cedar.

Gordon was pretty slow about everything he did. Ray told him, "I made my living by one tenth of a second and he had better speed up. That morning I had him feed some cubes to a big Brahma cow that had just had a calf. He got about half way to her and she charged him. He dropped that feed sack and ran like hell back to the truck. I told him I could see that he could move pretty fast."

Gordon eventually moved his wife and two daughters to Ray's ranch from England. Gordon's daughter recalls her time there when Ray would have been seventy three years old.

It was the fall of 1993 when my family and I moved from a small village in Northern England to the Cowboy Capital of the World. My parents had been given the opportunity to leave the cold damp life of English farmers and come to sunny Texas to work for one of the most famous cowboys of the day, Ray Wharton.

I was eight years old when my parents started working for Ray. I spent many hours in the roping pen listening to Ray holler and coach young calf ropers. Even as a young child, I could see the respect he demanded from everything and everyone in the pen, horses and cattle included. Many times I watched as these young men struggled with their horses in the box. It seemed like a completely different horse the moment Ray stepped up into the saddle.

What started as a battle between horse and roper quickly became remedied when Ray took the reins. Some people work their whole lives and still don't have the knowledge and talent Ray has. I truly believe the average horseman in a whole lifetime wouldn't understand the ability that just came so naturally to Ray. Some people are just gifted, a God given talent. This shined true not only as a world champion calf roper in his younger days but also as a 73 year-old who would crawl up in the middle of a rank horse who needed to be straightened out.

The time my parents worked for this cowboy I learned so much, including how to cuss. All I can say is they don't make them like they used to. When I think of the True American Cowboy, one man, Ray Wharton, will always come to mind.

Eleanor Prest Duke

Chapter 8

The Hunting Ranch

When Ray lived in Tarpley with his family there was no such thing as hunting leases. There really wasn't hunting just for the fun of it; you hunted for food. But forty years later it was big business in the Texas Hill Country.

Ray recalled his experiences in the development of the hunting industry in the Texas Hill Country:

In 1968, a banker friend told me that a woman named Stoddard wanted to lease her ranch west of Tarpley. I knew the Stoddards when they used to sit at my table at the Cabaret. I leased the ranch from her for a dollar an acre for five years. The ranch hadn't been hunted for several years, the roads were washed out, fences were down and everything was overgrown with brush.

I had these two big tractors from Bob Woodard and I knew I could run them. There were five of us that went to work on that place and before long we made a ranch of that place. I had to let one hard working boy go because he got to drinking. I told him he was a hard worker but when he drank whiskey he always screwed up. When I left Tarpley, I swore I would never have goats again, but had to put some goats on the lease to get rid of some of the overgrowth. The ranch had one house with two fireplaces and a big screened in porch across the front. It had a small shack near the barn on the place. Pappie stayed there a lot and fed the deer and turkeys.

I called Randy Moore to help me get hunters for the property and also a cook. I knew Randy from when he rode with me and Don McLaughlin. I told Randy I didn't want anybody except doctors, lawyers and politicians. I wanted only wealthy guys that liked to have fun. I

Hunting ranch in Tarpley, Texas.
Photo courtesy of the Whartons.

had to approve them and most of them were well to do. You can't imagine the great bunch of hunters I had. I had more fun there.

Randy brought James Slider with him to look at the property. Randy thought the sun set on Slider, but he was always riding me. Slider was a lobbyist. At first he said he was already on several hunting leases but when he found out it was Bandera, he said he was in.

Peyton McKnight, a state senator and Bob Bullock, the Texas Comptroller and later Lt. Governor also joined. Ikey Hart, Bill Aldridge (Halliburton Bill), Eddy Wallace and many others came on the lease. Randy brought his college roommate Peppy McKinney and Randy's dad, Big Randy Moore, Sr. Big Randy had played major league baseball with Casey Stengel and then for Casey when he was manager. Big Randy brought Bud, a colored fellow, to do the cooking.

I charged them each $150 whether they hunted or not. Most of them didn't come out to hunt. They came to drink, play poker and get away from their wives. The older guys stayed in town at the Lost Valley Dude Ranch. We all made trips to the Cabaret, the Silver Dollar, the Purple Cow and Jack Jones Steak House.

Then there were the doctors. They would all come the first week of hunting season. They would never go hunting but they came to drink and play poker away from their wives. Some wives tried to get their husbands to stop coming. Sam Wilson's wife finally got her way and made him stop. Sam and another guy brought their wives with them for the week. We were all down at the Purple Cow and I told them they had always made fun of how dumb I was, but I was smarter than the two of them. Now your wives are going to come down here and see what goes on in Bandera. You'll never get to come back to camp.

The politicians were a lot smarter than that. They didn't deer hunt much, but before they went home they

The "hunters" – best left unnamed to protect the innocent amongst the group. Photo courtesy of the Whartons.

would put on their hunting clothes and wallow in the dirt.

When we first started out there, they loved to hunt turkeys. I had moved Pappie out there and he would feed the deer and the turkeys. When James Slider was going to come out with Randy Moore to hunt turkeys, I planned a surprise for them. I caught and tied these turkeys that I had just bought from a lady in town and put them in a hallway in the barn.

I wasn't going to tell anyone, but Peppy, Randy and Ikey Hart, an older iron worker from East Texas, caught me with the turkeys tied up in the barn. I told them if they said anything about this at hunting camp, they would stop some bird shot in their back sides.

I put the turkeys in a horse trailer and took them to Tarpley, putting the trailer in a goat shed. That evening we tied one by the leg to the feeder pen where Slider was going to hunt. I told Bud, the cook, to come wake me when he heard Slider shoot. When he heard the shot he came in and told me, but I asked him to fix me a cup of coffee and we would sit there for a while and think what kind of lie Slider was going to tell. Bud and I knew Slider would take off the strings that had tied down the turkey. When we finally got up to go we saw Slider about 300 yards off, walking toward us. Slider didn't take his turkey to the screened in game room but hung it in a tree next to the house.

When Slider came into the house I told him that sure is a nice turkey and then asked him where he was when he shot the turkey.

"I was sitting there in the blind and just before daylight saw him up on the top of that hill and he gobbled and flew off that hill right into the feeder."

Soon everybody came in and Randy asked Slider how far that turkey flew. Slider repeated his story but when Randy asked him again, Slider blew up saying "You know how far he flew because you're the SOB that tied that turkey to the pen." We all went to laughing.

I let Slider believe that Randy had done it. When Slider was leaving, I told him he owed me for that turkey. He blew up again.

Ray tried the turkey trick again with Big Randy and an older friend of his who wanted a turkey. He tied two turkeys under a tree right off the road on the way to the front gate but the two men drove right by them. Ikey and Eddy came driving by, saw the turkeys and shot them. When they went to pick them up they saw that they had been tied. Not wanting anyone to know they had shot the tied down turkeys, instead of bringing them to the house, they took them back into Tarpley to the country store.

When the politicians came to the hunting ranch, they always ran around in Bandera. They made fun of my ninth grade education. One time three of them were arguing and worrying over something. It seems that one of them was being threatened with a paternity suit. I went up to them and told them that they didn't know how to get out of trouble. You're all so smart and gone to college and law school and now you're running the state. I can get you out of that problem in an hour or two.

Things went on for some time and finally one called me wanting to know if I could really help him with this. I told him to give me a day so I could find the right people. The next day I called back and said I wasn't going to give him any information unless he agreed to help me sometime in the future. He agreed but didn't want me calling him unless I really needed help. I told him I had a witness that knew the woman in question had a hysterectomy and so could not be pregnant now.

A couple years later I was being sued down at the lake and I needed a good lawyer. I called the man and he gave me the name of a Kerrville lawyer who happened to be related to the judge. I never had any more trouble down at the lake.

Randy was friends with Bud McFadden from their football days at the University of Texas. Bud was at the Oilers training camp in Kerrville and he, Bobby Lane, Charley Tolar, and Joe Childress wanted to kill a yearling buck and barbecue it. I told them they would have to pay the fine if we got caught shooting out of season. Bud said they would pay the fine. They killed a spike and when coming back stopped in Bandera for a drink. The deer was lying in the back of my pickup. Bobby was worried about someone seeing the deer.

"I ain't worried about that deer. You and Bud were going to pay the fine if we got caught."

Bud replied, "Ray, you get behind that steering wheel and let's go up to your house."

Another time four of the Houston Oilers were driving across Hondo Creek and water started coming in Ray's Pontiac Grand Prix. Ray cursed at them for being so heavy. One of the players said he wanted to buy his wife a second-hand car, but he was afraid he'd get one that Ray had owned.

Ray recalls an incident with Frank Rhoades. Frank called from Throckmorton, Texas, and said he wanted to go deer hunting. He had heard that Ray had a lot of deer and he was ready to come down and shoot one. "Tie up one of those bucks for me," were Frank's exact words.

I had just killed a deer and froze him whole. I got Bud and A. J. Lot to help me tie up that deer about 125 yards from the blind. When Frank came over, I drove up to where I had the deer tied. I said there's one, right there. Frank took out his lever action 30-30 saddle gun and shot one time and then shot again. The deer didn't move. Frank started to pump another bullet into the gun.

I stopped him saying, "Give me that gun before you run that deer off. I'll shoot him for you.'"

Frank reared up and hollered that he would hit him. I told Frank that there was no use him using up all his shells that we should just go over and untie the deer.

"Is that deer sure enough tied?" roared a very angry Frank.

"You told me to tie one up for you" was Ray's justification.

Big Randy brought a banker from east of Dallas to the hunting ranch. The banker flew into Hondo, mostly to play poker. Randy told Ray to be nice to the little guy because "he could buy us all with just his pocket money." Ray knew the banker had a "shiny" wife from the pictures he had showed them.

That night we went into town to the Cabaret. The little banker saw all these women there—some single, some not. He asked me where the husbands of the married women were. When I told him their husbands were off hunting, he got so upset and had me drive him back to his plane the next day.

Mrs. Stoddard died before the lease was up and the bank wanted Ray to lease from her son, but he decided against it.

"We all had too many good times at that place, too many to tell and some I can't tell." Ray said. "All of my hunters became some of my best friends. I'll never forget them."

Chapter 9

Honors and Reflections on a Life Well Lived

In March of 1982 Bandera honored their seven rodeo champions: Toots Mansfield, Ray Wharton, Buddy Groff, Clay Billings, Scooter Fries, Todd Whitewood, and Jimmy Adams with a monument on the Bandera County Courthouse lawn. All seven men were present for the dedication of the monument.

The men represented fifty-years of rodeo and Bandera history. Norma Anderwald designed the monument that includes a large buckle, a cowboy and of course the names of the champions. A commemorative buckle was given to each of the champions.

Photo of Ray and Buddy Groff at a ceremony honoring Bandera's rodeo champions. March 1982. *Photo courtesy of the Whartons.*

Ray with his "Gene Autry" hat courtesy of Nancy Bragg. Ada and Bill Hancock are pictured with them.

Ray, Shoat Webster, Gene Peacock and Nancy Bragg at the Old-Time Cowboys Reunion in Cimarron, New Mexico in 1994. *Photo courtesy of the Whartons.*

Ray and Ada settled into a more relaxed period of life with Ray buying a ranch in Batesville for some of his cattle and another ranch outside of Dilley.

"People don't want to see an old has been," commented Ray in 1984 when he was sixty-four years old. That was after a full day's work on his ranch as he was being interviewed by Tommy West when the Professional Rodeo Cowboys Association was returning to Bandera after a thirty year absence. Ray had performed in the last PRCA-sanctioned rodeo at Mansfield Park but he was content to be a spectator at this rodeo.

In 1993 Ray attended the groundbreaking ceremonies for the Museum of Champion Ropers on the grounds of the Roy Cooper Roping Complex in Childress, Texas. Sixteen of the twenty living world champions attended: Toots Mansfield, Don McLaughlin, Jim Bob Altizer, Dean Oliver, Glen Franklin, Chris Lybbert, Troy Pruitt, Fred Whitfield, Jeff Copenhaver, Dave Brock, Ernie Taylor, Rabe Rabon, Phil Lyne, Tom Ferguson, Roy Cooper, and of course Ray. For calf roping enthusiasts it was a once in a life-time experience.

Ada and Ray attended an Old-Time Cowboy Reunion in Cimarron, New Mexico, in 1994. They were joined by Shoat Webster, Bill Hancock, Gene Peabody and Nancy Bragg Witmer. Nancy presented Ray with a new Gene Autry hat very similar to the one Ray bought at Madison Square Garden in the 1950s. The group laughed as hard as they had when the original prank occurred.

Ray was inducted into the Rodeo Hall of Fame at the National Cowboy & Western Heritage Museum in Oklahoma City in 1994. At the induction ceremony, Randy Moore of Oklahoma gave the introduction:

> The definition of the words hustle, try and tenacity are all defined the same—Ray Wharton of Bandera, Texas . . . Ray won or placed at every major rodeo in the United States, was a World Champion, and a career roper who was very successful—always focused on winning. Now folks, I'm not saying that Ray was the epitome of smoothness or finesse in the arena. His

smoothness was more like an attack cat and his finesse in the roping arena was comparable to a heat seeking missile . . . Ray did not just slip in the door with this group of inductees. He came in with endorsements from such legendary people as Toots Mansfield, Don McLaughlin, Jim Bob Altizer, Shoat Webster, Lanham Riley and with the help of a little brown quarter horse (Brownie). Yes, sir, Ray came in once again sliding head first.

Randy Moore went onto say, "If there was a hall of fame for outstanding people in the arena of life, Ray would be a shoo-in."

The master of ceremonies, Clem McSpadden, commented on Ray's acceptance speech, "Folks, his speech was just like he roped—it was done in ten seconds flat."

Included in the appendix of this book are several letters that were written from rodeo greats who wrote in support of Ray, including Toots Mansfield, Lanham Riley and Don McLaughlin.(Appendix 2)

The Texas Senate recognized Ray with a Senate Resolution in May of 1995. The resolution recognized Ray's induction into the Cowboy Hall of Fame and for his numerous rodeo accomplishments.

Brownie, Ray's exceptional roping horse was also honored in 1995 in an article by Tuffy Cooper in the *Quarter Horse Journal*. Cooper named Brownie as one of his top picks for best horses in roping history. Cooper noted that Brownie did well in and out doors, long or short arenas and he did well with any rider. He made mediocre ropers do better. Cooper described Brownie as having a heart as big as a wash tub.

Ray and Ada have had to say goodbye to many of Ray's rodeo friends when they passed. The same camaraderie and humor was present even in death. Frank Rhoades, a good friend who had retired in Las Vegas, invited Ray and Ada to visit him. Frank had experienced some problems with his family so he had a favor to ask of Ray. Frank asked Ray to take his ashes to Red Rock Canyon and to spread them out in the canyon. Ray immediately agreed to take care of his friend's last wishes.

Texas Lt. Governor Bob Bullock congratulating Ray and Ada on Ray's recognition by the Texas Senate. *Photo courtesy of the Bandera Bulletin.*

Ray Wharton on the far right with Peyton McNight, Bob Bullock, Jeff Wentworth and Ada. *Photo courtesy of the Bandera Bulletin.*

S.R. No. 769

SENATE RESOLUTION

WHEREAS, The Senate of the State of Texas takes pride in recognizing Ray Wharton of Bandera, Texas, on his induction into the National Cowboy Hall of Fame in Oklahoma City on October 23, 1994; and

WHEREAS, Crowned the World's Champion of Calf Ropers by the Rodeo Cowboys Association in 1956, Ray Wharton won or placed at every major rodeo in the United States during his outstanding career; and

WHEREAS, Often referred to as the "Mighty Mite" of rodeo's calf ropers, Ray Wharton first began roping when he was a four-year-old by swinging nooses around goats in a neighbor's arena; at the age of seven, he suffered a bad fall and subsequent bone disease in his right arm and was threatened with the loss of his arm; and

WHEREAS, An individual of uncommon determination and perseverance, Ray Wharton regained the use of his arm, started roping again, and worked on ranches in the Bandera area; his first rodeo win was at Sabinal, Texas, and after 11 years of competition in rodeos, he won the National Western at Denver; and

WHEREAS, He became a roper of incomparable finesse and captured his World Championship at the Madison Square Garden Rodeo in New York City, crowning his highly successful career; and

WHEREAS, Famous for his stamina, strength, and talent in the rodeo world, Ray Wharton also became well known for his sincere and warm personality and his generosity in helping others; and

WHEREAS, A gifted athlete who overcame adversity to achieve his goals, Ray Wharton is an exemplary individual and a legendary figure whose life story is a model of tenacity for youths across the country; now, therefore, be it

RESOLVED, That the Senate of the State of Texas, 74th Legislature, hereby commend Ray Wharton on his outstanding achievements and extend to him congratulations on his induction into the National Cowboy Hall of Fame; and, be it further

S.R. No. 769

RESOLVED, That a copy of this Resolution be prepared for
him as an expression of esteem from the Texas Senate.

Wentworth

Armbrister	Henderson	Ratliff
Barrientos	Leedom	Rosson
Bivins	Lucio	Shapiro
Brown	Luna	Sibley
Cain	Madla	Sims
Ellis	Moncrief	Truan
Gallegos	Montford	Turner
Galloway	Nelson	West
Harris	Nixon	Whitmire
Haywood	Patterson	Zaffirini

Bullock, President of the Senate

_____
President of the Senate

I hereby certify that the above
Resolution was adopted by the Senate
on April 24, 1995. _____

_____
Secretary of the Senate

_____
Member, Texas Senate

When the time came, Ray and Ada went to the canyon. They immediately saw a large sign that read: "Do Not Pour Out Ashes in Red Rock Canyon."

Ada was terrified that they might get arrested, but Ray laughed, now knowing why his friend picked him. Frank knew Ray would do it regardless of any law he might be breaking.

Bob Woodard and Ray had been friends since Ray was in his twenties. When Bob was gravely ill, he visited Ray for the last time. Bob brought his bird dog with him, but asked first if he could bring the dog inside the house. Then Bob asked if Ada and his driver would go outside. Bob knew how much Ray enjoyed bird hunting. He offered to sell, really give, Ray a great big ranch. Ray thanked Bob but declined saying he just sold two of his ranches so he didn't need any money or another ranch.

In 1999 Ray was diagnosed with cancer. He and Ada valiantly fought that battle. With his sense of humor still very much intact, Ray started planning his funeral service. Remembering what Bo Chesson had said to him decades ago about not having enough friends to be his pall bearers and he would have to pay people to carry his casket, Ray asked the men he wanted for that honor well in advance and even bought black silk ties for them.

After each man agreed to be a pall bearer, Ray gave instructions on what they were to wear. One of the men thought that Ray's demise was imminent since his planning was so detailed. Every time the man would leave town, he checked with Ray and let him know his itinerary. Several years later, the man gave up this tactic and just asked Ray to let him know when he might be needing his black silk tie—not that he was impatient for Ray to pass, but he wanted to be sure he could honor his friend's request.

In 2002 Ray was inducted into the Texas Rodeo Cowboy Hall of Fame, at that time located in Belton, Texas, and has since moved to Fort Worth. (Appendix 3) He was also recognized in the Champion's Hall at the ProRodeo Hall of Fame in Colorado Springs, Colorado.

He might still have been saying he was an old has been in 2009 when he was the Grand Marshal of the Bandera rodeo, but he was having too good of a time to think about his age. This was part of Bandera's Frontier Times Museum celebration to create a Texas Heroes Hall of Honor. Ray being in the first group inducted into the Hall of Honor was a fitting tribute.

Ray continued his generosity and his sense of humor when George Sharman asked Ray if he would contribute to the Frontier Times Museum building expansion fund. George said he would match whatever Ray contributed. It was agreed that Ray and Ada would contribute $20,000.

A week later Ray called George and said he had a meeting with his accountant who told him that he could not contribute that amount. George graciously said he understood and that he hadn't told anyone about the amount. Ray let him think on that for a while and then said he couldn't do the $20,000 but he could do $40,000.

Overwhelmed, George thanked and cursed him as he realized Ray's sense of humor and loyalty to the museum had cost him an additional $20,000. Ray also donated his 1956 championship saddle and gold and silver championship buckle to the Frontier Times Museum.

When reflecting on his rodeo era and the current one, Ray had these observations:

> Rodeo today is not near the same as it used to be. In my day you could come up from nowhere; you didn't need sponsors. Now everything is more expensive—horses, trailers, the money needed to travel, and the entry fees. It makes it harder for beginners to start. Now it's big business where larger rodeos are not open to all. Casey Tibbs and I instigated the National Finals taking the top winners in each sport. We did that to try to help the up and coming fellows. Then we had mostly rodeo cowboys for the directors of the association; now there are just a few.
>
> I remember being asked once if I was a cowboy. I answered, No, I'm a gambler. I put my money up for the entry fee and then go out and try to beat everybody in

Ray Wharton, Grand Marshal of the 2009 Bandera Rodeo.
Photo courtesy of James Taylor.

Ray at a reception at the Frontier Times Museum, Bandera, TX when he was inducted into the museum's Texas Heroes Hall of Honor. *Photo courtesy of the Whartons.*

the world.

At ninety-four-years-old and after battling cancer for fifteen year, when his body fails him, Ray said, "I always thought a fellow had to pay for his bad days. I must be payin' now for living so long."

When reminded that his friend Whiz Whisenhunt promised that he was going to have "two shiny angels" waiting for him in heaven, Ray quipped "He may not be there."

Another friend for decades, Ray D'Spain, made these heart-felt comments about Ray and Ada:

> I have known Ray for a long time now and have personally seen him and Ada help out a lot of organizations and I know they have helped more individuals than even God Almighty can account for. He has made people count out every dollar due him and then gives them the shirt off his back. I know his reasoning was to make better individuals of the people he and Ada helped. There is no way of knowing how many times Ray helped someone out when they didn't ask for help and never expected the gift or the favor. Ray is truly a good hearted person to have a reputation of being so ornery. Ray had a hard life growing up and I believe he just assumes if it comes easy, it's not worth doing. The day Ray Wharton meets his maker, we'll all gather around talking about our memories of him. I'll have to have a bucket of Snickers bars because I know we'll be there a long—long time.

On better days, Ray tells Ada how much he has appreciated their life together and the care she has tirelessly given him. Looking back on his difficult youth and then his successes after that he is content.

"Everything I got is from rodeo. I've done everything I ever wanted to do. I had the best life ever."

"I've had the best life. I've done everything I wanted to do."
Photo courtesy of James Taylor.

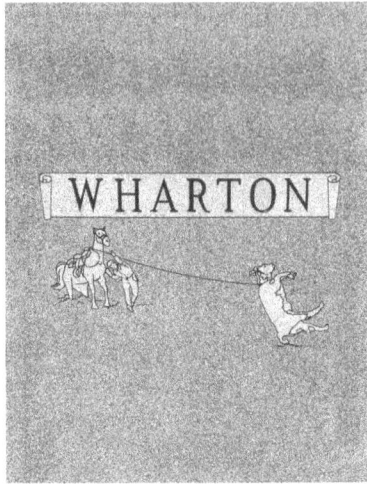

Epilogue

Ray Wharton passed away on October 20, 2014 at the age of ninety-four at his ranch in Bandera with Ada by his side. When Ada picked the date for the service, she knew Ray would not want it held on the weekend of the San Angelo Roping Fiesta. It was held the week after the roping event.

When Cody Ohl won the San Angelo roping, he asked that his winning rope be placed in Ray's casket as a tribute to the man who had helped so many ropers, himself included. Ada, of course, obliged knowing it would make Ray smile.

In the 1950s Bo Chesson joked that Ray was so ornery that he would have to pay his pall bearers to carry his casket. Ray's memorial service proved him wrong. Wearing crisp white shirts, black silk ties and Stetson hats that Ray had requested, fourteen pall bearers walked into the room overflowing with rodeo legends spanning six decades and his many friends. George Sharman officiated at the service where many laughed and cried, while he reminisced about their friend.

Ray D'Spain had a bucket of Snickers bars at the cemetery for friends to eat. Ada invited everyone back to their ranch where the reminiscing continued. Ray D'Spain's remarks summed up the feelings of many, "I hope he will be finding faster horses, good whiskey and long lost friends."

Appendices

Appendix I

World Champion Ray Wharton Honors Fellow Cowboys

It may have been a few years since 1956 RCA World Champion calf roper Ray Wharton of Bandera, Texas has roped, but he certainly hasn't forgotten those days and the great men he had the privilege of rodeoing with. Mr. Wharton made a very generous donation to the Justin Cowboy Crisis Fund in memory of those he roped with as well as those he served with in a leadership capacity as the RCA's Calf Roping Representative from 1957 to 1959. To see a full list of those he honored with his donation go to page 4. The photo above of Mr. Wharton ran in the March 15, 1957 Rodeo Sports News. Thanks to Mr. Wharton for his past leadership in rodeo and for his contribution that will assist many of today's injured rodeo athletes with their living expenses while they are unable to compete due to injury.

Reno Rodeo Lends a Big "Hand Up"

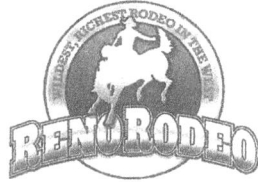

The 2012 Reno Rodeo was successful in every way - amazing crowds, spectacular livestock and, as usual, substantial funds raised for many charities. This year, the Reno Rodeo Committee designated proceeds from their 50/50 drawing to benefit the Justin Cowboy Crisis Fund. The total donation of $6,390 will certainly help JCCF fulfill the mission of giving "a hand up" to injured rodeo athletes and their families!

A COWBOY SAYS THANKS

Dear Justin Cowboy Crisis Fund,

Thank you so much for the incredible support you gave me during my shoulder surgery process. I've seen how much JCCF has helped cowboys over the years and always hoped I would never be in a position to need help myself. Your support helped me take the time necessary to heal completely, and it gave my family peace of mind while I was unable to rodeo. It has been a humbling experience to be shown such generous support in our time of need; thank you just doesn't seem to cover our true sentiments.

As a producer of the Kit Carson Pro Rodeo in Burlington, CO I am committed to having a silent auction with proceeds benefitting JCCF and we will make it an annual event. We want to do all we can to give back.

My goals are to be a great ambassador for the sport of rodeo, my sponsors and the Justin Cowboy Crisis Fund organization. Rodeo has allowed me to have my family with me on a daily basis, meet wonderful people and life long friends while making a living doing what I love. I am blessed to have such great support; I will always consider the Justin Boot Company and the Justin Cowboy Crisis Fund as family.

Thank you again,
Cory Wall
PRCA Bullfighter

JCCF DONORS
APRIL THROUGH JULY 2012

The Justin Cowboy Crisis Fund Board of Directors would like to extend their sincere appreciation to the generous donors who assist in giving injured rodeo professionals "A Hand Up."

JUSTIN BRANDS, INC
THE COWBOY REUNION, INC.
Taylor Global, Inc - Crown Royal
Helotes Festival Association, Inc.
Bob Feist Invitational
Dodge City Roundup Bounty Bull Program
Family Care Clinic Of Western Kansas, LLC • Kansas Orthopaedic Center, P.A.

Bob Tallman's Ranch Fixin's
California Circuit Finals Rodeo
Chuck Cundy
Cowgirl Regime
Doris Brogden
Dr. Jack and Elizabeth Smardo
George Terry
Harley Bates
Jean McPherson
Jeff & Carol Kinsey
Joe & Kristi Scelzi
John Pulling
Kevin Baxter
Lukacs & Associates
Mary Schlosser and Jeff Siddons
Neil Kirschbaum
Newmont Mining Corporation
Patricia Ludwig
Pikes Peak Hall Of Education Donations
Ramacco, Tony
Roger Schneider
Steven Ellrich
Taylor Global, Inc
Timberline Auto Center, Inc.
Tony Dentel
United Way Of The Columbia-Willamette

HONORARY DONATIONS
In Honor of Heber City PRCA Rodeo
Lazy J Rodeo Safety Equipment, LLC
In Honor of Sara and Steve Rempelos
Aje and Jennifer Sakamoto
In Honor of the Cheyenne Frontier Days Rodeo
Lazy J Rodeo Safety Equipment, LLC
In Honor of the Tri-State High School Rodeo Class of 2012
Mikey Duggan

MEMORIAL DONATIONS
In Memory of Anne Ziolkowski Christensen
Ruth Ziolkowski
In Memory of Bert Hamilton
Family and Friends
Ronald & Cassie Botts
In Memory of Betty Jean Thornton
Debbie Schroeder

In Memory of Bobby Soileau
Beau and Laura Mayo
Volf Enterprises
In Memory of Broc Cresta
Clayton and Kayla Foltyn
Gene Frank
Cathy Morgan
Steve and Sicily Orth
Spur Resources, Karen Herbst
In Memory of Carlie & Ty Anderson
Georgie Parenteau
Gary John & Janessa Parenteau
In Memory of Cathie Wright
Western Pacific Roofing Corporation
In Memory of David Elford
Paul and Avis McDaniel
In Memory of Dena Beck
Iden Bromfield
Timothy Green
Palomino Valley Wild Horse & Burro Center
In Memory of Diane Byrd
Western Pacific Roofing Corporation
In Memory of Jack White
Randy and Vicki Watson
In Memory of James "Jim" Gibbs
Thomas and Susan Lundeen
In Memory of Jesse Andrus
Sharon Allen
In Memory of John Banister
Western Pacific Roofing Corporation
In Memory of John Mason
Kerri Weaver
In Memory of John Zamrzla Sr.
Jeff and Dara Martin
California Collision Center
Oscar & Dawn Babers
Berglund Family
In Memory of Linda Pluss
Western Pacific Roofing Corporation
In Memory of Mike Hillman
Sharon Allen
In Memory of Phil Emfinger
Odessa Sandhills Stock Show & Rodeo
In Memory of Sandra Faye (Prichard) Vandiver
Randy and Vicki Watson
In Memory of Stan Immenschuh
Tom and Mary Lou Edwards

Ray Wharton made a generous donation to JCCF in Memory of these cowboys:

Amye Gamlin
Ben Johnson
Benny Adamietz
Bill Clendenen
Bill Hogue
Bill Linderman
Bill Mansfield
Bill Tiege
Billie Burns
Bo Chesson
Bob Mansfield
Bob Woodward
Bruce Mansfield
Bruce Montague
Buck Eckols
Buck Goodspeed
Buck Sorrels
Buck Telch
Bud Smith
Buddy Lytle
Bush Porter
Byrle Hartsell
Byron Wolford
C.D. "Tink" McCauley
Casey Tibbs
Charlie Montague
Chuck Sheppard
Clavin "Sonny" Greely, Jr.
Clay Billings
Clifton Lowery
Clyde Burk
Curly Thompson
Dan Poore
Dan Taylor
Dee Burke
Don Fedderson
Don McLaughlin
Doyle Riley
Dwight Graham
Ed Arnold
Ed Simms
Edward "Eddy" Akridge
Elmer Carter
Everett Shaw

JCCF DONORS
APRIL THROUGH JULY 2012

Ray Wharton made a generous donation to JCCF in Memory of these cowboys (continued)

Felix Billings
Frank Rhoades
Freddie Schmidt
Gene Clark
Gene Ramb
George Brown
George Epperson
George Teige
George Wilderspin
Gordon Davis
Guy Weeks
Harley May
Henry Fisher
Herb Dense
Herschel Romaine
Homer Pettigrew
Howard Billings
Ike Rude
Ira Reevis
J.R. Davenport
Jack Buschbom
Jack Riggs
Jack Saunders
Jack Shipworth
Jake Bogard
James Kenney
Jeff Revis
Jess Goodspeed
Jess Perkins
Jesse Burger

Jiggs Burke
Jim Bob Altizer
Jim Shoulders
Jim Snively
Joe Barnet
Joe Glenn
Joe Walters
John Eckhart
Johnny Leonard
Johnny Stevens
Juan Salinas
Junior Vaughn
L.N. Sikes
Lamar Hinnant
Lanham Riley
Larry Bowmar
Lee Cockrell
Lefty Wilkins
Lem Reeves
Leonard Block
Leonard Saye
Lewis Powers
Lex Connelly
Louis Brooks
Mack Yates
Mangum Sikes
Mansfield Autry
Marvin Hutto
Morris Witt
Pat Parker
Paul Bond
Paul Redden
Peppy McKinney

R.L. Bland
Raymond Hicks
Red Smith
Rex Beck
Rhea Mansfield
Richard Walker
Ronnie Sewalt
Roy Fly
Roy Matthews
Royce Sewalt
Shawn Burkett
Slim Whaley
Sonny Davis
Sonny Edwards
Todd Whatley
Tom East
Tom Nesmith
Tom Powers
Tom Taylor
Tony Salinas
Toots Hutto
Toots Mansfield
Troy Fort
Vernon Kerns
Vernon West
Walter Hicks
Walton Pogue
Waymond "Sonny" Groff
Whiz Whizenhunt
Willard Combs
Win Dubose
Windy Ryon
Zeno Farris

100%

ONE HUNDRED PERCENT OF YOUR TAX DEDUCTIBLE CONTRIBUTIONS TO THE JUSTIN COWBOY CRISIS FUND IS AWARDED AS DIRECT FINANCIAL ASSISTANCE TO INJURED RODEO ATHLETES AND THEIR FAMILIES DURING THEIR RECOVERY TIME FROM RODEO INJURIES.

Please accept my contribution of $ _____ to the Justin Cowboy Crisis Fund.
Name: _____
Address: _____
City: State: Zip: _____
_____ Check enclosed
_____ Please charge my credit card cc#: _____
Expiration date: _____ 3 digit security code: _____

My gift is being made in memory or honor of (circle one if applicable please)

_____
with acknowledgment card sent to: _____
Address: _____
City: State: Zip: _____

Please mail your contribution to: **Justin Cowboy Crisis Fund**
101 Pro Rodeo Drive, Colorado Springs, CO 80919
Items for silent and live auction fundraisers are also accepted

Official Charity of the

Appendix II

RANDY G.
MOORE

PRESIDENT
RANDY MOORE OIL & GAS, Inc.
(903) 884-2125
(903) 884-2525

December 15, 1993

Rodeo Historical Society
National Cowboy Hall of Fame
1700 N.E. 63rd Street
Oklahoma City, Oklahoma 73111

Re: 1994 Rodeo Hall of Fame

Dear Committee Members:

Ray Wharton was a "Study of Tenacity." His focus was to give all out effort on each and every rodeo run. His competitors have stated that he gave 110% every time he 'nodded his head.'

Ray's desire to win was complimented with two other easily recognizable traits. One was his unselfish generosity to help fellow ropers with horses, calves, food, money and a place to stay. The other characteristic so warmly received was his genuine and enjoyable personality.

After Ray's championship season in 1956 and his eventual retirement from PRCA competition, he continued his champion efforts in other endeavors. Success as a horse trainer, rancher, lake realtor and investor exemplified his continued desire to excel.

What more could a selection committee want than a tenacious competitor with a lovable personality who has generously helped his many friends along life's trails.

Sincerely yours,

Randy Moore

Randy Moore

RANDY MOORE OIL & GAS, Inc.
℅ RANDY MOORE RANCH
HWY 259 NORTH
P.O. DRAWER 607
OMAHA, TEXAS 75571

RANCH (903) 884-2100
RESIDENCE (903) 884-3040

October 4, 1993

Rodeo Historical Society
National Cowboy Hall of Fame
1700 N.E. 63rd Street
Oklahoma City, OK 73111

RE: 1994 Rodeo Hall of Fame

Gentlemen:

Please regard the enclosed as a formal request to
consider Ray Whorten, Bandera, Texas, as a 1994
Rodeo Hall of Fame Honoree.

I've known Ray personally for many years and a
more dedicated cowboy and rodeo fan you'll never
find.   His life has been spent around rodeos and
rodeo people, they are his first love.

I would be very proud to have Ray join our ranks.

Sincerely,

Shoat Webster

Shoat Webster

Letter From Toots Mansfield

Big Spring, Texas
October 30, 1993

The Rodeo Historical Society,

Dear Sirs:

   Would you please consider my good friend Ray Wharton
for induction into the Cowboy Hall of Fame.
   He is more than deserving of the honor and I think
that he would be an excellent choice.

Thanks very much,
yours truly,

Toots Mansfield

*The handwritten letter had faded over the years and was not clear enough
for printing. His signature remained legible.*

Letter From Don McLaughlin

I roped against Ray Wharton for many years. We also traveled many miles together rodeoing in the same vehicle. To me, Ray Wharton was one of the most fierce competitors I've ever competed against. The bigger and the wider the calves were, the tougher he was. Ray was liked by all ropers and was always ready and willing to give a helping hand. This along with Ray's roping ability to me makes him a shoe-in for the Cowboy Hall of Fame in Oklahoma City,

Sincerely,

Don Mc Laughlin

Don McLaughlin with Ray Wharton.

The Rodeo Historical Society
National Cowboy Hall of Fame
Oklahoma City, Oklahoma 73111

To the nominating committee:

I respectfully submit Mr. Ray Wharton as a nominee for
induction into the National Cowboy Hall of Fame. In
1943, I first met Ray at a roping held in Ozona, Texas.
His display of "hustle" and "try" caught my attention.
No calf was too wild or too large for Ray to handle.

Ray represented the calf ropers on the RCA board of
directors in the mid 1950's. He was World Champion Calf
Roper in 1956. Some of the best calf roping horses
of that era were trained, owned, and ridden by Ray
Wharton.

Ray was known for his loving approach but he was quick
to assist any cowboy down on his luck, no matter what
event he worked.

I feel that Ray's roping skills, his outstanding
character, and love of the sport should be honored by
our Hall of Fame.

Sincerely,

Appendix III

TEXAS RODEO COWBOY HALL OF FAME
COWBOYS WORKING FOR COWBOYS
YESTERDAY - TODAY - TOMORROW

CONTACT:
DWAYNE (D. L.) MEACHAM,
PRESIDENT-CEO

302 LAFAYETTE LANE
LEAGUE CITY, TX 77573
281 316-0704
281 316-6932 FAX

VOLUME 2, ISSUE NO. 1, MAR- APR- MAY, 2002   GENEVIEVE WEYER, EDITOR

CONGRATULATIONS
☆ **2002 HALL OF FAME MEMBERS** ☆

2002 HALL OF FAME CHAMPIONS: L TO R on front row accepting for **LAWRENCE CAREY** - deceased. 2nd from left on the front row is **J. R. AKRIDGE, KAY THURMAN** accepting for her son, **BRENT THURMAN** -deceased, **WANDA BUSH** and Na**RAY RATLIFF**. Back row L TO R accepting for **ROYCE SEWALT** -deceased, accepting for **TOOTS MANSFIELD**-deceased. Third from left on the back row is **GRADY ALLEN, EDDY AKRIDGE, DELBERT HATAWAY, EUGENE JOHNSON, DICKIE RICHARD, WACEY CATHEY, QUAIL DOBBS** and **RAY WHARTON**.
(PHOTO BY DUDLEY BARKER 254 968-3433)
Not shown but definitely represented was the large delegation of members from the **CLAY   COUNTY PIONEER REUNION   AND RODEO ASSOCIATION** from Henrietta who was awarded the **SPECIAL RECOGNITION AWARD.**

Bibliography

Carroll, R. D., *Shoat A Champion Roper*. Barnsdall, OK, Evans Publications Inc., 2003.

Cooper, Tuffy, Specialty. *The Quarter Horse Journal*, Aug 1995.

Davis, Ray, Ray Wharton Rope Horse Trainer, *Western Horseman*, Jan 1971.

Mahoney, Sylvia, Roy Cooper Breaks New Ground, *Western Horseman*, Nov 1993.

Mangold, Lanham, 1956 World Champion Ray Wharton: The Best Darn Cowboy That Ever Did Ride. *Loops Magazine*, Oct 2003.

Mansfield Taught 'Em, Bandera Boys Top Ropers. Express and News, Oct 21, 1956.

Porter, William H., Ray Hurries. Ft Worth, TX, *The Cattleman*, Volume XLIII, No. 1, June 1956.

Pruett, Gene, Cowboy Association. National Cowboy Hall of Fame, Volume IV, #1.

Richards, Rusty. *Casey Tibbs Born To Ride*. Wickenburg, AZ, Moonlight Mesa Associates, 2010.

Rhodes, Ruth, Rodeo… 'Round the Rena'. Bandera, TX, *Dude Wrangler*, April 1956.

San Antonio Express and News, Ray Wharton: King of the Calf Ropers. Feb10, 1957.

Schumacher, M. J., *A Pictorial History of Bandera County: 150 Years of Challenges and Courage, Champions and Characters*. Virginia Beach, VA, Donning Company Publishers, 2006.

Van Winkle, Irene, Whartons Paved the Way before Camp Verde's Camels Roamed; *West Kerr Current*, Ingram, TX, Aug 1, 2009, Feb 25, 2012 and June 12, 2013.

West, Tommy, Rodeo On Its Way Back, Trails West, *San Antonio Express*, 1985.

Woerner, Gail Hughbanks, *The Cowboy Turtle Association: the Birth of Professional Rodeo*, Eakin Press, Fort Worth TX., 2011.

Woerner, Gail Hughbanks, *Rope to Win: The History of Steer, Calf and Team Roping*, Eakin Press, Fort Worth TX., 2007.

Woerner, Gail Hughbanks, Colonel W. T. Johnson: An Extraordinary Showman. *ProRodeo Sports News*, Volume 56-No.24/Dec 26, 2008.

Index

The Authors

George Sharman was raised in Bandera, Texas. George is a 1970 graduate of Texas A&M. He worked as a general contractor in Houston for thirty years before returning to Bandera. When he returned to Bandera, he rented a place owned by Ray Wharton for six years. George and Ray knew each other for about forty years. George now has his own ranch in Bandera County and is an active supporter of the Junior Livestock Show and the Frontier Times Museum. George started taping his weekly conversations with Ray and soon realized that his story is a part of rodeo and Texas history. His knowledge and respect for Ray, the history of the area and his enthusiasm for the western way of life make him the perfect person to oversee this project.

Editor-Dr. Maggie Schumacher retired to Bandera, Texas, in 2002 after working for Penn State University for 28 years. She has her degrees from Pennsylvania institutions: Bachelor's from Immaculata College, A Masters from Shippensburg State University and her Doctorate from the Pennsylvania State University. Since living in Bandera she has edited and wrote several chapters in *The Pictorial History of Bandera County*, created the winning design for Bandera's city flag, and served on Bandera's city council. She has written historical pieces for local newspapers and developed programs on Women of the West-their clothing, cowgirl history, rodeo cowgirl history and early Texas Hill Country female artists and writers.

www.ingramcontent.com/pod-product-compliance
Lightning Source LLC
Chambersburg PA
CBHW071350090426
42738CB00012B/3076